Meet Me at the Station

Meet Me
at the Station

Elizabeth A. Willmot

Gage Publishing

Gage Publishing
© Elizabeth A. Willmot

Canadian Cataloguing in Publication Data

Willmot, Elizabeth A., 1918-
    Meet me at the station

    Includes index.
    ISBN 0-7715-9976-5

    1. Railroads—Ontario—Stations.
    I. Title.

    TF302.058W54   385'.314'09713   C76-017148-3

Designed by Fortunato Aglialoro

Printed and bound in Canada
1 2 3 4 5 AP 80 79 78 77 76

Introduction

On the Christmas before my fifth birthday, an event took place which influenced my entire life. With my parents, we five children boarded the train at the old Toronto Union Station and headed north for Aurora where we would celebrate Christmas at the farm of our grandfather, Mancel Willmot. Details of the journey are vague except for our arrival in Aurora. Even through the eyes of a small child it was a picture postcard scene at the railway station that night. Passengers stepped out onto the snow-covered wooden platform, calling greetings to friends – and there in his wonderful horse-drawn cutter was my uncle who had come to meet us at the station. The sound of the jinga-jinga-jing of the sleigh bells added further excitement as we sped between the deep snow banks along the country road.

There has always been a magical quality in railway stations for me ever since that Christmas so long ago. With my first camera I began photographing old steam locomotives, the people who worked for the railway, and of course, railway stations.

Because of my deep affection for the railway, I experience great sadness when I see the changes in railroading in my lifetime and I feel as though an old friend has gone whenever a favourite railway station is demolished. Through writing and photography I have strived to arouse an awareness throughout Ontario of the importance of the preservation of historically important railway stations. How rewarding it is when I hear that another lovely old railway station has been restored, and given an opportunity to retain its dignity in the community while serving in a new role.

This book has been written for people who travelled during the days of steam engines, and who remember the joy of anticipation when they called out, "Meet me at the station!"

AT THIS PLACE ON MAY 16 1853 THE FIRST TRAIN IN ONTARIO HAULED BY A STEAM LOCOMOTIVE STARTED AND RAN TO AURORA

YOUNG WOMEN
TRAVELLING ALONE

Do not start for a strange city or town, even for a night, without previous information of a safe place to stay.

Do not ask or accept information, advice or direction except from railway officials or the Travellers' Aid.

On Arrival in a Strange City

If you are alone,
If your friends fail to meet you,
If you wish the address of a reliable hotel or boarding house,

Look for the woman at the station wearing the Travellers' Aid badge.

Canadian Badge

United States
National Badge

LOCAL REPRESENTATIVE

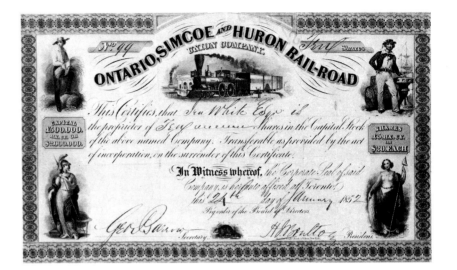

ONTARIO, SIMCOE AND HURON RAIL-ROAD

G. T. R. Sys.	ONE WAY
Form 1. ●	LOCAL
681	*aurora*
	(Destination of Ticket)
	Fare $
11-11	**STUB—Not good for passage**

G. T. R. Sys.	EXCURSION
Form 1 X. ●	LOCAL
1191	*Davenport*
	(Destination of Ticket)
	Issued on date stamped on back
	Returning *Jan 3* 19 15
	Fare $
10-12	**STUB-Not good for passage**

FIRST STEAM TRAIN 1853

On May 16, 1853, the Ontario Simcoe and Huron Union Railroad Company operated the first steam train in Canada West from Toronto to Machell's Corners (Aurora). The train, consisting of four passenger and freight cars was drawn by the steam engine "Toronto", the first locomotive constructed in what is now Ontario. The arrival of the railway accelerated the development of this community, which was incorporated as a village in 1863 and a town in 1888. With the opening of this section of the railway one third of the proposed line was completed. Begun in 1851 and completed in 1855 the railroad was built to connect Lakes Ontario and Huron from Toronto to Collingwood.

Erected by the Archaeological and Historic Sites Board,
Department of Public Records and Archives of Ontario

Aurora *First Steam Train 1853*

"On May 16, 1853, the Ontario, Simcoe and Huron Union Railroad Company operated the first steam train in Canada West from Toronto to Machell's Corners (Aurora). The train, consisting of four passenger and freight cars was drawn by the steam engine "Toronto", the first locomotive constructed in what is now Ontario. The arrival of the railway accelerated the development of this community, which was incorporated as a village in 1863 and a town in 1888. With the opening of this section of the railway one third of the proposed line was completed. Begun in 1851 and completed in 1855 the railroad was built to connect Lakes Ontario and Huron from Toronto to Collingwood".

Years of suspense-filled drama preceded that historic event which is recorded on an historical plaque erected at the CN station in Aurora and a bronze plaque at Toronto Union Station.

An entirely new industry was started when construction was begun on the Ontario, Simcoe and Huron Railroad in 1851. Few people were qualified to direct the operations. There were no bulldozers or steam-shovels to perform the heavy tasks. All work had to be carried out by inexperienced labourers. There were no locomotives, or places to build them, and no steel for tracks.

Despite the obstacles, in just eighteen months after the beginning of construction, a passenger train was able to steam out of Toronto on May 16, 1853, and head for Machell's Corners.

To officially initiate the beginning of the railway's construction, Lady Elgin,

wife of the Governor General, turned the first piece of sod and placed it in a miniature wheelbarrow. At this ceremony, which took place in front of the Parliament Buildings in Toronto, there was an estimated crowd of over 25,000 in attendance, such was the enthusiasm over the beginning of construction of this first railway.

Sandford Fleming (who later became Sir Sandford), one time chief engineer of the Ontario, Simcoe and Huron Railway, preserved a piece of the sod lifted at the ceremony. Some time later it was presented to the Royal Canadian Institute where it remains today. In an exquisite wooden inlaid box lined with cerise satin the sod is encased beneath glass.

From Toronto, the railway line went in a westerly direction as far as the village of Parkdale before turning to the north. In October 1852 a steam locomotive was brought by ship from Oswego, New York, to Toronto harbour, and in that same month, it was given a trial run of the line which had now reached the village of Concord, 14 miles north of the city.

By the middle of April 1853 the first steam locomotive ever to be built in Canada, had been completed in the foundry of James Good on Queen Street East in Toronto. This little locomotive suitably named "The Toronto" was designed, as well as built, by Mr. Good. His original drawings show a pair of Gothic windows in the cab of the locomotive, four high driving wheels, four truck wheels, and an enormous smoke stack.

On the morning of May 16, 1853,

crowds gathered in front of Sword's Hotel on Front Street to witness the historic moment when passenger railway service would begin. The majority of these people had never ridden on a train, and it is probable that only a few had ever seen one.

Tickets for the 30 mile trip to Machell's Corners (now Aurora) cost $1, an amount considered scandalous by some critics. The journey took two hours, and at its destination, a hero's welcome was given engineer William Huckett who was also master-mechanic of the railway. To honour the arrival of the steam engine era colourful celebrations took place in Toronto and Machell's Corners, concluding with a gigantic display of fireworks. The tiny community of Machell's Corners which had been named after it first merchant soon changed its name to Aurora. Now that it had a claim to fame in railway history it seemed time for an appropriately dignified name.

Following the building of a railway station on Wellington Street, Aurora's development began in earnest. Soon there were two hotels, a grist mill, tannery, a wagon maker, coffin maker and a brewery. The community became a village in 1863, and was incorporated as a town on January 1, 1888.

The present station in Aurora was built in 1900 by the Grand Trunk Railway which had taken over the railway in 1888 by amalgamation. Four passenger trains ran each day, plus frequent excursions to Toronto and the popular picnic area at Bond Lake. Passenger service today is reduced to morning and evening

Dagmar CPR

commuter service.

The simple design of the railway station is relieved by an attractive porte-cochère on the north end of the building. A fretwork design, created within the three gables in the roof, appears to be symbolical of Aurora, the Greek Godess of Dawn. Possibly the lines radiating from the central disc were the carpenter's interpretation of the dawn's rays of light.

Railroad timetables make fascinating reading! You wonder about the imaginative names and the stories behind them. One of the most intriguing lists of station names is found along CPR's Havelock subdivision, beginning at Glen Tay. When you say that name, you can almost smell the heather and hear the skirl of bagpipes.

Continuing to the west along the line you approach Mountain Grove – such a cool sounding name – then there is Kaladar, Tweed, Ivanhoe, Bonarlaw – all names with great character.

Down the line after passing through Peterborough, Havelock, Cavan and Pontypool, you arrive at the smallest operational station on that line. Little Dagmar, about 25 miles east of Toronto, is just a flag-stop. From the station you see fields of grain and stands of timber, but when you follow the gravel road to the north, suddenly you are surrounded by magnificent skiing country.

During the thirties and forties, CPR ran special weekend ski trains to Dagmar. An open sleigh pulled by two great Percherons met the trains and carried skiers off for a day on the slopes. By late afternoon the tiny waiting room would be packed with people clustered around the pot-bellied stove. Sandwiches, left over from lunch and toasted over the coals, tasted heavenly!

Furnishings are sparse and crude in the station. A plain unpainted wooden bench runs around the walls – and that's all there is. A storm door keeps out the icy blasts in wintertime.

Sheltered from the elements by sweeping branches of weeping willows, Dagmar, the comical little "boxcar red" station, still serves the community. Each morning, one or two commuters stand on the gravel platform, ready to flag down the Toronto-bound train.

Inglewood

An aura of elegance embraces the term "union station." With it we associate Greek pillars, Gothic arches, and a history of visiting royalty. Surely a little frame station up in the Caledon Hills could hardly merit this title!

There was once a union station on a high plateau overlooking the Credit River and valley at Sligo Junction (now Inglewood). In the late 1870s, the tracks of the Hamilton and Northwestern Railway, and the Credit Valley Railway converged, and crossed one another at this point, thus making it a union station – of sorts. Eight passenger trains a day, and numerous freight trains kept the station agent as busy as his urban counterparts.

It's too late to see this union station. It was destroyed by fire around 1910. The yellow brick station which was built to replace it was demolished in 1972, several years after the cessation of passenger service in this part of Ontario. All that remains in the area to remind us that this used to be a busy railway centre, is the red wooden water tower, just to the north of the diamond-crossing of the two tracks. The station hotel which was so popular with travelling business men is now a private residence.

The Credit Valley Railway's time table of 1883, refers to Sligo Junction as Riverdale. Because another town in Ontario was also called Riverdale, this name was changed to Inglewood.

A daily way-freight still uses the line built by the Credit Valley Railway (now CPR), but the other tracks which were taken over by Grand Trunk, before finally becoming a part of CNR, have long since been abandoned.

Mr. Robert "Chummy" Smeaton and his friend Edgar "Dixie" Ireland, both lifelong residents of the village, will never forget the occasion when the night operator at the station became inebriated and fell asleep on the job. His responsibility was to know the exact location of every train in his subdivision, and to give clearance orders to the crews to proceed from station to station. The station agent had to sort out the confusion, and before he finished, it looked as though trains were backed up from Inglewood to Toronto! Every lad in the village stayed at the station that night to watch the fun.

For Mr. Smeaton and Mr. Ireland, the station was their clubhouse right from the time of early boyhood days. No other place in the village could offer such a variety of entertainment. Their usual routine each evening was to drop in to the general store, buy a box of soda crackers and a tin of sardines, and sit on the platform, munching this nightly treat while watching the passing rail traffic.

Every morning at 9:15, the Grand Trunk's mixed-train picked up high school students at Inglewood and took them to school in Georgetown. Conductor Darsh wouldn't tolerate any nonsense on his train. When children became boisterous, they were banished to the smoking car where they had to sit in silence.

Coaches used on these mixed trains were of the style used in the old colonist trains. Some had wooden seats, while others had stiff red plush, which had a way of working through your clothes, and causing a good case of the itch. If the windows were opened on these coaches, a fine cloud of black soot soon found its way inside where it settled on everything and everyone. Kerosene lanterns, with their unforgettable aroma, provided a subdued illumination.

"Dixie" Ireland remembers going to the station in time for the arrival of the early morning freight train so that he could get the day's weather report. Grand Trunk provided a novel weather forecasting service for rural communities. On the side of the train, a board would be marked with one of three symbols. A full moon indicated fine weather – a half moon meant showers – and a single star was the forecast for anything from a good downpour to a hurricane.

The Inglewood station was the source of probably the first piped-in music which ever found its way into a railway station. Freddie Martin, the night operator in the early 1920s, used to fill in his spare time at the station, playing his fiddle. "Dixie" Ireland would bring in his bass fiddle, and Jack Ramsay joined them with his banjo. The trio invited the night operator at Allandale to tune in on their concerts, and soon, night operators from Toronto to North Bay were sending in requests for their favourite music.

What an important part of community life railway stations played in Canada's past – and when we see pictures of these old buildings demolished now, it is surely sad to think that no reminder is left of a wonderful Canadian way-of-life for the generations to come.

Craigleith

On Nottawasaga Bay, a few miles west of Collingwood, you can still see the Craigleith station which was built more than one hundred years ago by Ontario's first railway company, the Ontario, Simcoe and Huron Railway. The name of the company had been changed in 1858, and by the time the tracks were built through Craigleith, it was called the Northern Railway of Canada.

When it was built in 1872, it served a booming lumbering village which rejoiced when rail transportation became available. The village and area rapidly became a favourite holiday site, and summer trains were filled with travellers. When skiing became popular, resorts were developed on the surrounding hillsides, and special ski trains shuttled back and forth between Toronto and Craigleith. At any time of year the station was busy. By 1966, skiers and summer tourists had almost totally abandoned the easy way of travelling in favour of using their own cars, and so the station inevitably was forced to discontinue service. But there is a happy ending to the story.

The station was bought by Mr. and Mrs. Ken Knapman who converted it into a combined museum and restaurant. The exterior is kept in a perfect state of restoration, and is painted in the original railway red. It's pleasant to think of the old waiting room in the station still crowded with travellers and skiing enthusiasts.

Every season reveals its particular beauty in Craigleith. Perhaps for many the favourite time is spring when the wild lilac bushes surrounding the station bloom in profusion and fill the air with their sweet fragrance. But for those who admire the beauty of winter, the station would have a tremendous appeal. Because it was built in the very heart of a snowbelt, great drifts of snow all but conceal the station from the roadway, and when snow drifts curl over the eaves and cling to the red shingles, the station resembles a cake decorated in boiled icing.

The land on which the station was built was originally owned by Andrew Fleming, father of Sandford, who later became Sir Sandford Fleming. It was he who persuaded his father to donate the land to the railway.

Residents in the community are proud when they speak of this great man whose proposal of world Standard Time in 1878 brought international unification of the method of time determination. One can only guess at the aggravation experienced by the railways before Standard Time was adopted. When each community had its own standard, the setting of railway schedules must have been a nightmare.

In the early days of the railways it was customary to honour visiting dignitaries by decorating railway stations along the route of travel. Flags, flowers and bunting set the theme, and when Albert Edward, Prince of Wales, son of Queen Victoria, came to Canada for a visit in 1860, villages vied with one another in their choice of extravagant decorations. Almost every station between Toronto and Collingwood had erected spectacular floral arches beneath which the young prince would pass in his open observation car.

In 1974 when a special excursion train carrying hundreds of railway fans retraced the route taken by the young prince, a member of the planning committee suggested a revival of the delightful old custom of the floral arches. However, only Craigleith decided to put up the arches. With the profusion of lilac blossoms at the site, how could the venture fail? Fate did not smile on that excursion! In an attempt to hold back the lilac blossoms, they were stored in the local apple storage plant. On the evening before the train trip, post diggers went to work with enthusiasm and dug deep holes to support the tall arches. Quite by accident, the cable which controlled railway signals for miles along the line was severed. Bedlam ensued! Warning bells and flashing red lights operated out of control for at least the next twelve hours. To compound the miseries, a heavy rainstorm blew in off the bay during the night after the lilacs and boughs of cedar had been fastened around the archway. By morning, the blossoms were a sodden mass – the rain still fell – and with relentless repetition bells rang and lights flashed at every level crossing.

Photographers didn't succeed in getting worthwhile pictures of the lilac bower, as the storm increased in intensity throughout the day. It's doubtful that officials of any town will ever again be persuaded to participate or even discuss the revival of the floral arch.

Maple CNR

An old railway station which hasn't had a fresh coat of paint in over thirty years, and hasn't seen a passenger in its waiting room for almost ten years, does not often get the opportunity to experience "the second time around."

The exception to this rule occurred at the Maple railway station in 1974 when commuter service was introduced between Toronto and Barrie. Suddenly Stephen Campbell, veteran agent-operator at Maple, was surrounded by painters, railway officials, new tickets and time-tables. His quiet old station suddenly came to life.

Curls and blisters of ancient railway-red paint were scraped from the surface of the vertical board-and-batten station, and over the handsome old building was applied the new favourite railway station colour – gray with bright blue and red doors. Probably it's an improvement, but somehow its appearance suggests an aging lady whose dignity has been lost by the use of cosmetics unbecoming to her years.

The comforting old pot-bellied stove in the waiting room was replaced with a modern electric heater, and along the walls modern posters are displayed. Whatever became of the pictures of ships which were sailing for foreign lands? Or the advertisements of Harvest Excursions to Winnipeg? Or the prominently displayed "Advice to Young Ladies Travelling Alone?"

Maple's station stands on that historic railway track built in 1853 by the Ontario, Simcoe and Huron Railway Company. This company became known as the Northern Railway of Canada in 1858, and in 1888 it became amalgamated with the Grand Trunk Railway, which, of course, became a part of the CN system in 1923.

The first railway station in the village was in use until October 1905. It was destroyed by fire caused by the head-on collision of two trains in front of the station. It was reported that while the two engineers argued about who was to blame for the accident, a burning box car toppled over against the tinder-dry station, and in a matter of moments, the entire building was ablaze.

Stephen Campbell operated the Maple station for many years prior to his retirement in 1975. He and his family had lived in the simple frame cottage provided by the railway company, which matched the station with its coat of railway-red paint.

The railway had always been Steve's life. His father had been station agent in Palgrave, and all during his boyhood years, Steve remembers listening to the wonderful stories told by his grandfather who was an engineer for the Grand Trunk.

Anyone who lived in Maple during the steam era, will remember the story about the engineer who adjusted the whistle on his locomotive to play a recognizable tune. At the same time every day, villagers stopped whatever they were doing to listen for the arrival of the train. When the short steam ditty echoed through the village, the unseen audience would nod and say, "There's old Tuney."

Mr. William Ingram, the village postmaster was a favourite visitor at the railway station in the days when the mail came up on the train. The history of Maple and Vaughan Township had become a hobby of his, and his tales of the early days were always interesting to hear.

The Maple Station is probably the last remaining Grand Trunk Station having mileage stencilled on the name board hanging above the bay window of the station office. The wording on the south end of the board is "Toronto 18 miles," while at the north end is "North Bay 197 miles." This feature was also remembered in the sign on the station at King City, and at Stayner. It was apparently unique with Grand Trunk stations.

The station which Steve Campbell tended for so many years is a fairly busy place again. The parking lot is always filled with commuters' cars. Steve enjoyed hearing conversation in the waiting room after the years of silence after passenger service was discontinued. Along this main line of the Canadian National Railway, there is a constant flow of freight trains, and twice a day, the Supercontinental streaks past the old station.

Lorneville Junction

The Lorneville Junction station isn't an easy one to find today. There are no railway tracks in the area. It used to sit at the junction of the Midland Railway line where it crossed the Toronto and Nipissing Railway about 15 miles east of Lindsay. Now it's resting behind Mr. Elmer Jordan's barn, surrounded by lilac bushes and farm machinery.

The Toronto and Nipissing Railway was pressed for funds by the time their line reached Lorneville, and the strained budget couldn't pay for fancy railway stations. The station at Lorneville Junction was similar to others along the line – vertical board-and-batten with a shingled roof – a small waiting room dominated by a squat pot-bellied stove – a baggage room, and an area where the station operator-agent could sit and conduct his business. The exterior of all these old buildings was identical. Each one was given a coat of "box-car red" paint which faded and peeled.

When the Lorneville station was in use, the majority of passengers using the waiting room were those who had had to change trains to reach Beaverton. Their trip from Toronto took practically the entire day. After their train deposited them at the junction station, they had to wait for the arrival of the Midland Railway train which came from Lindsay. Passengers from Cannington and Woodville who wanted to travel to Lindsay also had to disembark at Lorneville Junction and wait for the eastbound Midland Railway train to complete their journey.

It was along this Toronto and Nipissing line that an old Fairlie locomotive used to labour in the 1870s. It was usually referred to as a two-headed monster. Certainly it was a freak, but still it was named "The Shedden" to honour the president of the railway.

Someone who saw the Fairlie described her as being "like a two-headed monster fiery dragon, belching sparks and billows of black smoke from both of its huge smokestacks. This double-header roared or crawled through forests and farms of the backwoods country until one day it exploded." Railroading back in those times had its problems, but left a heritage of colourful yarns for us to enjoy.

At the time of the demolition of the Woodville railway station, Mr. Victor Heard salvaged old freight ledgers and records of the Grand Trunk Railway and the Toronto and Nipissing Railway. Woodville is the first town to the south of Lorneville on the original Toronto and Nipissing line. The contents of these ledgers revealed much about the habits of the people who lived almost 100 years ago. Each item was entered in the ledger in elegant copper-plate script which would do justice to any graduation certificate. In a column marked "Species of goods," contents of orders were listed along with names of recipients, and the cost of shipping. During the first eleven months of the year you could see that few unnecessary goods were ordered. The most common items were egg cases, salted fish, sugar, coal oil, farm machinery etc.; but all that changed in the early days of December. You could sense the mounting excitement as you scanned each page of the ledger. There were orders for mincemeat, fancy cakes and biscuits, pails of candies, raisins and nuts, whiskey in barrels, coconuts and oranges, and boxes of silks and lace trimmings. The aroma of Christmas pervaded the station freight room at this time of year.

If ledgers from Lorneville and all the other little stations along the line had been kept, they would have been almost identical in description and content.

The last train to pass through Lorneville Junction was on November 3, 1958, and was the Lindsay to Midland freight train. Tragedy marred the day when the train collided with a car at a level crossing, killing the occupant, Mrs. Fred Smith.

When rail service was finally concluded and the tracks removed, Mr. Elmer Jordan who had been a track foreman with Canadian National Railways, bought the station and moved it to his farm. Although the station had no claim to beauty, still it had its own charm.

Abandoned right-of-ways can still be recognized in the area, and right on up to Coboconk which was the northern terminus. They, and the little frame station marked "Lorneville" are almost all that is left to remind us of that early Ontario railway, the Toronto and Nipissing.

Streetsville

A strong back was a prime requisite for settlers in the early 1800s in Ontario. But almost more important was the possession of courage and confidence about the future. Timothy Street who settled on the Mullet Creek in 1819, where the village of Streetsville was built, must have had all of these qualifications. He could walk the 21 muddy miles to the grist mill in York (Toronto), or prod his team of oxen along the way. By building his own grist mill in 1821, he eased, to a degree, the transportation problem.

Fifty-eight years later, Timothy Street's village was rewarded for its confidence and patience, when the newly built Credit Valley Railway brought its line from Toronto through Streetsville in 1879.

It is interesting to discover the types of business undertakings which flourished in these remote settlements in the days when transportation was limited to stage-coaches, ox carts, or horses. In Streetsville's early days there was a Mr. T. Cartwright whose specialty was making plug hats! There were two millinery shops, a broom and pail factory, a carriage shop, a mercantile business operated by Gooderham and Worts, general stores, as well as grist mills and sawmills.

The village blacksmith, Josiah Bennett, was a railway enthusiast who couldn't wait for the railway to come to him. When he heard that the Grand Trunk Railway would be passing through Georgetown, north of Streetsville, and that they would be building an iron bridge across the Credit River, it was like the song of the siren to him. He packed his tools and forge onto the ox cart and headed north where his skill as a smithy could be used by the Grand Trunk in the construction of the bridge which is still in use today.

Friday, September 19, 1879 was a day to be remembered in Streetsville – the occasion of the formal opening of the Credit Valley Railway. Most of the villagers were present at the new station at the Junction when the train passed through town on its way to Milton where a formal reception was to be held. Queen Victoria's son-in-law, the Marquis of Lorne, Canada's Governor General at that time, officiated at the opening ceremony. Invitations to the guests read as follows:

MARQUIS OF LORNE
OPENING OF THE
CREDIT VALLEY RAILWAY
by HIS EXCELLENCY
THE GOVERNOR GENERAL
Friday 19th September 1879
The Credit Valley Railway Company
Requests the pleasure of your presence
on the occasion of
The opening of the railway by
His Excellency the Governor General
on Friday the 19th inst.
Train will leave Queen St. Station
at 9.45 A.M. precisely
And will return to that station at 1 P.M.

It was 10:55 A.M. when the train departed from Toronto, and at 11:25 A.M. it passed through Streetsville. The occasion which started off so joyfully, was marred by tragedy when Mr. Gooderham of Streetsville, who got off the train to see why it had made an unscheduled stop, fell beneath the wheels and was killed when the train began to move again.

Streetsville had two railway stations initially. A small frame station was in the centre of the village, and has been gone for many years, but the street name "Old Railway Street" recalls its presence. The tracks divided at the Junction on the northern outskirts of the village. One line went on to St. Thomas, while the other terminated in Orangeville, 56 miles north of Toronto. This particular line passed through Brampton, Forks of the Credit, Church's Falls, and Alton before coming into Orangeville. A branch line cut off at Church's Falls, and along a 27-mile route, passing through the villages of Erin, Hillsburg, Fergus and terminated at Elora.

The white frame station with its circular tower which sat at the Streetsville Junction from 1879 until 1914 was a busy spot. There were four daily passenger trains in both directions on the St. Thomas line, and two in each direction on the Orangeville and Elora lines. Probably the busiest man in town was the driver of the horse-drawn bus which met each train and took passengers to Streetsville's hotels.

The CPR took over the Credit Valley Railway in 1909 and built a new brick railway station in the heart of town. The old station at the Junction was closed, and in 1914, Mr. Ephriam Evans bought and moved it to William St., directly behind the present station. Whether or not Mr. Evans was a railway enthusiast is not known, but his tremendous respect for his new home was quite obvious.

Mr. and Mrs. McBride Hunter, the present owners, also share his nostalgic feelings about the delightful old railway

Milton CNR

station. Their bedroom was once the station agent's office, above which was the turret where the telegraph operator sat. Patterned wooden ceilings remain in each room, and the original time-worn doors still hang. Twenty-one panes of 5 inch square pebbled glass form an interesting detail in the upper portions of the double-hung windows. The old waiting room became the dining and kitchen areas, and the freight room is now the family living room.

When the Credit Valley Railway built their station at the Streetsville Junction in 1879, it was recognized as one of the prettiest along the entire line. It is indeed pleasant to see this beautifully preserved old railway station being used and enjoyed by people who respect its history, and who strive to keep alive the memories of its origin.

"They've come to take us out of the mud!" Those were grateful words in Milton when the Hamilton and North-Western Railway's first train steamed into town on October 3, 1877.

Before that time anyone wanting to travel by train, first had to hire John Marshall's stage coach to be taken to Acton, Georgetown or Oakville. The fare for this leg of the journey cost 87½ cents. During spring and fall stagecoaches were usually axle deep in mud, and frequently all thoughts of travelling had to be abandoned until the roads either dried in the sunshine, or froze up.

The tiny settlement founded by Joseph Martin on October 15, 1821 made practically no progress until the arrival of the railway, because of its inaccessibility. By 1879 the village had two railroads when the Credit Valley Railway brought through its line.

History repeats itself in Milton. Passenger service on both lines had been discontinued to Milton, and once again, one must go to Oakville or Georgetown to catch a passenger train.

Fortunately the CNR's attractive station with its abundance of shapely gables, is serving the community in a new capacity. The Chamber of Commerce bought and moved the building to Unity Park on the edge of town, where it has been converted to a tourist bureau.

The interior of the station illustrates the skill of carpenters in the 1800s. Narrow vertical boards stained a rich brown provide an unusual and attractive covering for the waiting room walls. A heavy wooden cornice imparts the final touch of richness to the room.

The station still wears its seasoned coat of "box-car red" paint – that traditional colour in railway history.

Petrolia CNR

A carpenter recently crawled through the trap door leading to the unused area of the tower of the Petrolia railway station and was astonished by the superb craftsmanship. The beams are solid oak, and look as though they could stand for another hundred years. Even though those carpenters who built the station so long ago, knew that the upper portion of the towers would never be revealed for inspection, still their utmost skill was applied to every remote detail.

This handsome red brick-and-stone station, built by the Grand Trunk Railway in 1903 is a study in Victorian grandeur. On each end are circular turrets complete with bellcast roofs, and graceful supporting brackets. Carved finials crown the peak of each turret. Above the front door with its fan transom, stands a square tower with a lovely Palladian window in the front elevation and arched windows on two sides. Long sidelights brightened up the vestibule, and on each side of the main entrance are square windows glazed with an artistic weblike design.

Beneath the turrets, circular waiting rooms were built; one for the ladies and the other for gentlemen. The circular theme was carried out in every detail in these rooms. A continuous curved bench was molded to the shape of the walls. Glass in the three six-foot long windows was unusually thick, and curved to the same degree to follow the line of the walls. A magnificent spiralled ceiling was added to proclaim the ultimate touch of elegance. These two waiting rooms were finished in a rich dark oak. The centre portion of the station housed the usual general waiting room, the ticket office, operator's desk at the back of the building, and a baggage room at one end.

A stranger visiting Petrolia today would not recognize that the railway station is now a library. Although it has served in this capacity since March 25, 1937, the exterior still remains as it was built over seventy years ago. The conversion of this station to its present use, is probably the first Canadian example of an unused railway station being preserved by a town and put to an appropriate use.

When this station was built, it replaced the Grand Trunk station which had been built by the Great Western Railway on the original track brought into Petrolia in 1866. Pictures of the old station show a sombre two-story frame building without artistic embellishments. A town which in 1866 became Canada's first "oil capital," surely deserved a more pretentious railway station.

Petrolia is on the Bear Creek in Lambton County in southwestern Ontario, and was originally named Enniskillen. However, in honour of the discovery of rock oil in 1861, the name was changed to Petrolia. Few towns in Canada have experienced more exciting boom conditions than those which occurred in Petrolia. After the Civil War in the United States, Americans began investing heavily in the newly discovered oil fields. Kerosene was soon being distilled in Petrolia, and tallow candles and whale-oil lamps were discarded in favour of this modern way of lighting.

During the first five years of the oil boom, the need for a railway in Petrolia was desperate. Ox-carts transporting enormous barrels of oil were a common sight on the main street. But the railways were not yet convinced that the oil supply would warrant the cost of running in a spur line to the town. However, when the famous King well came in at 800 barrels a day in 1866, the town could wait no longer for proper transportation. They financed and built a spur from the town of Wyoming into the heart of town. The line was so successful, that the Great Western Railway bought and operated it until the time of the amalgamation with the Grand Trunk Railway in 1882.

Trains coming into Petrolia have always had to back down the five-mile spur line. This track comes to an abrupt end a few yards from the back door of the station, which is the terminus of the line. Frequently its proximity has been a source of consternation. On September 29, 1965, two box cars roared down the tracks completely out of control and only an act of providence stopped them from careening right through the back wall of the library.

For Mrs. Jackson who began working in the library in 1937, the building has a special, nostalgic meaning. She attended high school in Petrolia, and had to come to school by train from her family's farm near the Plympton-Enniskillen town line. Every day after 4 o'clock the station looked like an annex of the high school when most of the out-of-town students sat in the comfort of the station and got started on their homework while waiting for the train's return.

Train crews were very accommodating to country students in those days. Whenever they saw a child running across the fields carrying a lunch pail and school bag, they stopped the train and waited. Not only school children were treated with this courtesy. Farmers' wives frequently would fill a basket with eggs and butter to be sold in town, and by just waving a white handkerchief, they knew that the train would stop for them.

Mildred Jackson's father always waited with her for the arrival of the train on stormy winter mornings. He would carry a gasoline lantern which he used as a signal for the train crew. The rapport between rural students and the railway was like that of a big comfortable family. The engineer and conductor knew who lived on every farm along the route, and knew how many children they should expect to pick up each day.

Ever since 1959, Mrs. Jackson has been in charge of the library, and even though she has a busy schedule, thoughts of her high school experiences and memories of the old station still return. The old ticket office and operator's window is now the space for her office. The baggage room has been converted into the children's library, and the ladies' waiting room now serves as a library boardroom.

Although the railway hasn't used the station for almost thirty years, there is still an unmistakable aroma in the lovely old red brick building – a faint trace of coal smoke – a hint of kerosene – yes, it's all there – and probably always will be.

Flag Stops in Rural Ontario

Dotted about rural Ontario there used to be a rash of miniature railway stations which appeared on time-tables preceded by "f." Locomotive engineers slowed down when approaching these stations to watch for a summoning by someone waving a green flag, or lighted lantern – even a handkerchief was sufficient! Usually these miniature stations were comical with ornamentation inappropriate for their size, while some occasionally had a small touch of refinement. Travellers enjoyed poking fun at these little stations, but would be incensed if the station were abused or ridiculed by outsiders. Because of their size, flag stations seemed to arouse a protective spirit in those whom they served.

Forks of the Credit
In the 1880s passengers travelling north from Toronto on the Credit Valley Railway were treated to spectacular scenery, and equally spectacular engineering skill in bridge construction. The most outstanding bridge spanned the west branch of the Credit River at the Forks of the Credit. This amazing wooden structure was over 1000 feet long and stood 85 feet above the river. After crossing this bridge, the train stopped at the small frame station known as "Forks of the Credit." The station met a tragic end when senseless vandals shoved it over the side of the gorge.

Goderich CPR

Long before there ever was a Huron County, or the shores of Lake Huron had been settled by Canadian pioneers, there was a large encampment of Chippewa Indians at the mouth of the Menesetung River (now the Maitland River).

In 1827, this site was chosen for a settlement which would be called Goderich. Its existence was due to the energetic and imaginative planning of John Galt, the Scottish novelist who directed the development of the Canada Company in the Huron Tract. This crown land, comprising more than one million acres of virgin forest, extended from Lake Huron to Guelph.

It was John Galt's close friend, Dr. "Tiger" Dunlop who chose the exact location for the new settlement on Lake Huron, and under his direction, a road was cut through the forests to the present site of Guelph. Along this same route, the Canadian Pacific completed their railway on August 26, 1907, joining these two early communities of the Canada Company. Goderich built around a central octagonal hub immediately became a unique settlement because of its design. The central portion was a well-treed, grass-covered area where the town hall and market place were built. From it radiated eight roads on which the villagers built their homes. This plan probably appealed to Galt and Dunlop because of its similarity to styles they had known in their home towns in Scotland and England, with the village green, or hub as it was in Goderich, recognized as the focal point of the community.

Settlement of the area took place gradually due to difficulty in transportation, but with the arrival of the railway in 1858, there was a dramatic surge of settlers. The Buffalo and Lake Huron was the first railway to come to Goderich. Their line was completed on June 28, 1858, thus establishing a direct overland route between Lake Erie and Lake Huron.

Mr. Joseph Whitehead, a pioneer in railroading, was active in the construction of many sections of the Buffalo and Lake Huron Railway. He was regarded by many as somewhat of a celebrity because of the fact that he had been the stoker on Stephenson's locomotive, the "Rocket" when it reached the incredible speed of 29 m.p.h. in 1829. This achievement had convinced the Liverpool and Manchester Railway that steam would work.

The contribution of the railway toward the development of Goderich became more apparent when vast deposits of salt were discovered in the vicinity in 1866. Since that time, long freight trains have been transporting more than a million tons of salt each year.

Like so many other Ontario towns today, Goderich no longer has railway passenger service. Its two handsome railway stations are now operated for freight dispatching.

When you study the unusually lovely design of the CPR station which overlooks the harbour of Goderich, you feel that it is regrettable that crowds of passengers are not here to enjoy it. Every detail of the two-story station indicates that it was built to be admired. When the CPR built the station in 1907, railway architects had graduated away from their early timid approach to railway design.

The four tall windows in the circular waiting room provided an excellent view out over the harbour, or one could watch the activity at the round-house. A shingled conical turret, rising high above the roof ridge, attractively capped this end of the building. A striking entrance to the station from the platform was created by narrow sidelights on each side of the door, with an elliptical fan transom spanning the entire unit. This same theme was repeated over the bay window of the office area. In the gable of the roof, an attractive grouping of a set of eight small-paned windows were arranged in a semi-circular pattern.

The Canadian Pacific Railway station at Goderich is certainly conclusive evidence that Canadians achieved originality in railway architecture. The preservation of this strikingly beautiful station is indeed desirable as a part of our heritage.

Belleville CNR

Belleville's railway history ran the full scale from famine to feast in a very short period of time. Up until 1856 it didn't have a single railway, and within a few years, no less than five companies ran lines through the town.

The railway era began with a great flourish in Belleville when it became a divisional point on the newly completed Grand Trunk Railway in 1856. This brought about the building of a car-repair shop, a large roundhouse and business office, as well as the railway station.

Belleville's second railway was the Grand Junction, built in 1878. It was a 33 mile line running through Campbellford, and Hastings, terminating in Peterborough.

In 1879 the Belleville and North Hastings Railway was completed to the village of Madoc. This was an extremely important little railway, as it provided a means of transporting iron ore from the mines in North Hastings county to Belleville's harbour on the Bay of Quinte. These two small railways became amalgamated with the Midland Railway Company of Canada, and then with the Grand Trunk Railway, before becoming a part of the Canadian National system.

The fourth and fifth lines to be brought through Belleville, the Canadian Northern and the CPR, shared the same railway station.

In 1856 the Grand Trunk Railway built the station which is used today by the Canadian National. It represents the influence of French architecture in railway station design. The lower portion of the building is a continuous pattern in cutstone. On the facade, a series of five arched windows is surrounded by wedge-shaped stone vousoirs and a handsome pattern is created at each corner of the station by the irregular placement of stone quoins. An attractive group of dormer windows with ornamental curved heads above the frame, project artistically from the mansard roof. The entire effect is so pleasing that it seems strange that this design was not put to greater use by the Grand Trunk Railway.

East of Belleville the lines of the Canadian National and Canadian Pacific Railways run a parallel course, and in some areas are scarcely more than an arm's length apart. To the crews of steam locomotives, this presented an irresistable challenge. There was a silent agreement that a race would take place between the Montreal-Toronto trains which departed from Montreal at the same time each day.

Mr. Herbert Stitt of Toronto who fired for Canadian Pacific during the steam years recalls his role in these rousing contests. Much of the speed of the train depended on the ability of the fireman to keep a hot fire. His engineer would have one eye on his opponent, and the other on the pressure gauges, while he constantly shouted at his fireman for more steam. Passengers leaned out the coach windows, waving hats and handkerchiefs and cheering on their crews. Even the farmers along the way were caught up in the drama. The trains pulling up to sixteen coaches would have exceeded 80 miles per hour during the race! This was indeed the Queen's Plate of the railway!

On an occasion when an engineer was being reprimanded by a railway official for breaking company rules by participating in these contests, the lecture was concluded with, "But don't ever let me hear of our competitors beating us!"

Similar anecdotes fill the history of the early days of the railway. Many of the stories were known only to the train crews who were a part of an incomparable phase of Canadian history.

When the Grand Trunk built its main line from Montreal to Toronto, the railways were very much in their infancy. However, their Belleville railway station, regarded as magnificent in 1856 when it was built, is still considered one of the most outstanding examples of Canadian railway architecture.

Georgetown

How casually we accept the marvels of modern transportation! After seeing the first man walk on the moon, our enthusiasm is spent when the feat is repeated. We've become so nonchalant, that in the progress of transportation, nothing strikes us as being miraculous or spectacular. But back in 1837 if a stage coach arrived in Hungry Hollow on schedule (now Georgetown), that was miraculous. When the Grand Trunk Railway arrived in the village in 1857, that was spectacular!

Deplorable road conditions existed around Georgetown, and expansion of the village was slow indeed. Would-be settlers hesitated to start out for an area which was isolated by incredible amounts of snow during the winter months, and axle-deep mud in the spring and fall.

The Grand Trunk line to Georgetown from Toronto was built primarily for the movement of freight, with little preparation made for the comfort of passengers. Only extremely crude accommodation was available in the early days. Box-cars were fitted out with wooden benches nailed to the floor. With the absence of windows in these cars, along with the uncomfortable seats, little could be said about the benefits of train travelling except that it was faster than walking.

These conditions were soon rectified and passengers sat on varnished wooden seats in proper coaches. Wicker seats were introduced later, and finally the plush upholstered seats appeared. Although in appearance they provided a touch of elegance, they were always associated with the itch they produced in anyone whose trip took longer than an hour. The hard-wearing material had a way of penetrating through every layer of ladies' petticoats – even through heavy underwear worn beneath men's serge suits.

In 1877, The Hamilton and Northwestern Railway Company completed its northern extension which ran between Hamilton and Barrie. The line passed through Georgetown, adding further importance to the railway junction.

Georgetown has always been proud of its railway bridge which was built by the Grand Trunk Railway in 1857. This 768 foot-long bridge was supported on limestone piers, 112 feet in height. It was completed at a cost of $500,000, and for more than 120 years it has carried all the rail traffic passing into the town.

Bridge construction had not reached the highly technical level used today, and blacksmiths performed most of the construction of the Georgetown bridge. Josiah Bennett, the village blacksmith in Streetsville, was one of the men who came to work on the bridge.

The Grand Trunk built their Georgetown railway station with the same cutstone which was used in their bridge. Quarries at the nearby village of Limehouse provided the stone which imparts a feeling of strength and great character to this handsome station.

The architect's plans for the station show the usual office, and separate waiting rooms for ladies and gentlemen. Still another waiting room was available for anyone wishing to smoke. In the frame tower with its interesting octagonal roof, the telegraph operator had his quarters, where from a group of five windows he had a fine view of traffic along the line. In the gable above the bay window of the ticket office carpenters created an attractive wooden fan-shaped pattern. A long frame porte-cochère at one end of the station has been dismantled for some time.

Frequent train excursions departed from the station, and were extremely popular during the 1800s. Usually they were one day trips, with occasional weekend trips to Niagara Falls. Posters in the waiting room urged farm boys to travel to Western Canada to help harvest the crops, and the fare for these excursions was just $12 to Winnipeg.

Grand Trunk officials in the early 1900s were unaware of the fringe benefits they made available to one young Georgetown couple during their courting days. Their homes were on the GTR line, but separated by several miles. Nightly visits were made possible when the young man found that he could ride on the caboose steps, and jump off when the train arrived at the backyard of his lady friend's home. At around 10 P.M. the same way-freight train returned, and the accommodating engineer gave a few warning toots on the whistle, giving the youth just enough time to streak through the screen door, hop the fence and catch the caboose railing.

Georgetown's railway station is still in use today, providing commuter service to Toronto. Although many changes have taken place in its function and design, it still represents a fine example of Ontario railway architecture.

Blyth CNR

In the early 1870s Patrick Kelly of Blyth, who owned a sawmill and door factory, had grown impatient with the necessity to haul his products 11 miles to the nearest railway station in Clinton for shipment. If his business was to continue, and the village to develop and prosper, it must have a railway connection.

Mr. Kelly discussed his problem with officials of the Great Western Railway in Hamilton who assured him that a line could be built if he could raise financial guarantees from the communities in the area between Wingham and Clinton.

His proposal for a railway was accepted enthusiastically, and the required sum was soon guaranteed. A subsidiary company was formed by the Great Western, and they called it the London, Huron and Bruce Railway. The line originated in London and continued northwesterly through Clinton, Blyth, terminating in Wingham, a total distance of 74 miles.

"The mixed-train" plied back and forth in a casual manner for 65 years. Adherence to a rigid schedule was of little importance to passengers or crew. Engineers agreeably stopped the train anywhere along the line to accommodate passengers. When it was noted that most passengers seemed to be carrying a basket of butter and eggs for the market in London, the train became affectionately known as "The Butter and Egg Special."

The railway was operated by the Great Western which was amalgamated with the Grand Trunk Railway in 1882, and the final operation was taken over by the Canadian National systems in 1923.

On Saturday, April 26, 1941 the train made its last trip following the announcement of the CN that the section between Clinton and Wingham was no longer profitable for the company. It was a sad, quiet trip for passengers on that last ride. Most people sat by the window of the coach, watching for the last time, the passing of each familiar landmark along the line. A short time later the tracks were removed, thus closing an era with finality.

When you drive through Blyth today, it's a startling experience to suddenly come upon this tiny frame railway station, standing well back from the road and surrounded by a field of tall grass and wild flowers.

While you are looking at the little station, you receive a strange sensation. The windows of the waiting room beneath the conical roof take on the appearance of two solemn black eyes peering out from beneath the brim of a witch's hat, and gazing constantly down a neglected right-of-way.

Tremendously appealing, the design of the station is ideally suitable for a rural community. Every detail is imaginative, revealing the pride and skill of early carpenters. Passengers sat in a circular waiting room, above which rose the steeply pitched conical roof. Three curved windows provided a view of the activities on the station platform, as well as an opportunity to watch for the approaching train.

Jutting out from the roof above the ticket office and baggage room was a small bay window which was probably purely ornamental. In some stations, however, a small room was built in the roof on the station, and the telegraph operator sat up there in front of his key and sounder.

When the Blyth CN station was closed, it was bought by a resident of the town, primarily for nostalgic reasons. In its perfect state of preservation, it seems almost a memorial to a nearly forgotten railway, the London, Huron and Bruce Railway Company, and the communities it served along its short line.

Stouffville CNR

Conversations with life-long residents of small rural communities frequently produce fascinating tales of local history. The origin of Stouffville goes back to 1802 when Abraham Stouffer and his friend, Peter Reesor, decided to emigrate with their families to Canada from Pennsylvania.

Peter Reesor consented to investigate available property, and set out for Toronto (then York) by horse. He was directed to land in Markham Township where he chose a site for his own family presently known as Cedar Grove. On his return to York, an ex-army officer approached him and asked if he would be interested in buying 400 acres in Whitchurch Township (present location of Stouffville). When Peter explained that he was not in a position to buy the land, the officer offered to trade it to him for his horse and saddle. The deal was closed and Peter returned to Pennsylvania on foot where he gave a glowing description of the rich farmland and dense forests in the area he had seen, and soon, the two families made their way in horse-drawn carts to Canada.

Abraham Stouffer chose a site 8 miles north of Cedar Grove in Whitchurch Township where he bought 200 acres. He cleared the land, built a dam, a grist mill and a sawmill, and soon other settlers were attracted to this community called Stouffer's Village. On July 1, 1877, it became incorporated as a village', and its name was changed to Stouffville.

The presence of the narrow-gauge Toronto Nipissing Railway which passed through Stouffville in 1871, was an important factor in the development of the village and surrounding area, as farmers developed a profitable business selling timber to the railway for fuel for their locomotives.

Stouffville soon became acquainted with the hazards of the early railroad when an explosion occurred on "The Shedden" an unusual type of locomotive known as a Fairlie. This double-ender woodburner had two separate fireboxes operated from one central cab. On January 31, 1873, one of the boilers burst, killing most of the crew, and causing great damage to the railway station. Repairs were made to the "Shedden" and it continued to serve the railway in its distinctively temperamental manner. A second explosion occurred in 1879, and in 1881 the locomotive was dismantled and put out of use.

Stouffville became a busy railway junction when a branch line was built in 1877 to Sutton, 26 miles north, by the Lake Simcoe Junction Railway. The Toronto and Nipissing Railway was acquired by the Midland Railway of Canada in 1882 and then by the Grand Trunk Railway in 1884. It was this last company which built the present station in 1886. It is a grey, two-story frame building with living quarters for the station agent and his family.

John Mason, operator-agent and his family lived in the Stouffville station from 1911 until 1932. His children remember how their friends seemed to gravitate to the station because of all the wonderful places to play. Climbing the old wooden water tower was a favourite sport, and the hand-operated turntable was usually covered with children taking rides while others pushed. For the adults election night at the station was one of the most exciting nights of the year. Every man in town gathered in the waiting room to hear the election results as they came hot off the wires of the telegrapher's table.

The design of Stouffville's station is austere, and yet there is appeal in its simplicity. The narrow white barge board relieves the plain lines of the roof, and in the triangle at the peak of the gable a wooden sunburst effect was added. Along the barge board around the bay window of the office, the carpenter also added a slight, ornamental flourish with his fret saw.

Many miles of the historic old narrow gauge railway which ran through Stouffville are now gone. The original route began in Toronto, went north to Stouffville, Uxbridge, Blackwater Junction, Cannington (where the sod turning ceremony had taken place), on through Woodville, Lorneville Junction, Eldon, Kirkfield and terminated at Coboconk. However, today all tracks have been removed north of Blackwater. The line now swings east at this point and goes along up to Lindsay and Fenelon Falls and terminates in Haliburton.

The last towns with passenger service today on the old Toronto Nipissing Railway line are Unionville and Stouffville. A commuter train takes passengers to Toronto in the morning and returns in the early evening.

Glencoe

Long before the Wright brothers had made their first historic flight near Kitty Hawk, Canada had an "AirLine." It was opened on July 26, 1873, and was a branch of the Great Western Railway. This early "AirLine" was just 146 miles long, and it joined Fort Erie with Glencoe in southwestern Ontario. History records that a few other countries had these early "AirLines," and the term usually applied to a railway which ran in an almost straight line from terminus to terminus.

The CN station in Glencoe today is composed of many familiar architectural details which found favour with the Grand Trunk Railway which had built the station circa 1890. Above the bay window where the telegraph operator sat, there is a steep gable. An octagonal turret rises above the roof ridge with an attractive bellcast roof sweeping out below it. A quadrangular window in the waiting room offered a pleasant place to sit and watch activity on the station platform. The interior walls are lined with tin, upon which was stamped an attractive geometrical floral design.

Frank Riley, who was station agent in Glencoe from 1939 until his retirement in June 1962, will always remember his first day at the station. It was June 6, 1939 and the royal train carrying King George VI and Queen Elizabeth was due to stop for a few minutes. After the train had taken on water, it would then proceed to Toronto. Thousands gathered at the station to see the royal couple. A pilot train preceded the royal train throughout the entire trip and was known as "Passenger extra 6401." The royal train was "Passenger

Extra 6400." Frank Riley still has the train orders which he had to issue to the engineer and conductor on 6400. The message on the flimsy paper read:

"Passenger extra 6400 East Glencoe Passenger extra 6401 East left Glencoe at ten forty one.
1041 P.M." (signed) Riley

This served as confirmation for the royal train that the pilot train was still in the lead and on schedule.

Life as a station agent in Glencoe was rewarding, and after his retirement, Mr. Riley continued to live in the town. When you meet Mr. and Mrs. Riley, and hear their tales of railroading, you realize that the railway governed their entire way of life. They both loved every aspect of the work, but felt that an era had come to an end when CN steam locomotive 6043 made its final run through Glencoe on April 28, 1960. The Rileys' home is a short distance from the main CN line, close enough that they can hear all the activity at the station, the shunting, crossing whistles and so on. The sound they miss most of all is the lusty shrieks of old steam locomotives.

After Frank Riley returned from active duty in the signal corps in World War I, he found employment with the Grand Trunk Railway as a relief station operator. He can rhyme off the 159 names of the stations where he worked like someone reciting a catechism: Cargill, Chesley, Hanover, Port Elgin, Kincardine. . . . He recalls that the "whole danged town used to come down to see the train go through at Cargill." And in

Goderich you always knew that old Tom Schwartz and his horse-driven "hack," the town's only livery, would be alongside the platform at train time to escort travellers up to the Bedford or the British American Hotel.

When he was agent in Wingham just after the war, Riley helped Wilf Cruickshanks build his radio station CKNX. In those days, radios were usually "crystal sets," and a little wire antenna, known as a "cat's whisker" would be deftly moved around the crystal until suddenly, as if by magic, the exciting sound of some distant radio program would come through your earphones. After CKNX was established Mr. Riley acted as a talent scout for a noon-day program called the George Spotton Hour. Shows were all live, and you could usually count on hearing a violinist or a vocal quartet on the Spotton Hour. After being a relief operator for almost twenty years, Mr. Riley welcomed the opportunity to settle down in one place.

Mr. Riley doesn't often visit the old station, but when Christmastime approaches he can't resist going back to see if the old atmosphere still exists. It was always a time of excitement with people returning home for the holidays, and the platform piled high with extra freight orders and luggage. Three or four extra men had to be employed to handle the work load, but high spirits prevailed despite long hours.

This line has been owned by the Canadian National for many years, but to the Rileys and most old railroaders, it's still the "AirLine."

Neustadt CNR

It's too late to see Neustadt's "box-car red" railway station. It was demolished in the mid 1970s, but Miss Charlotte Weinert who has always lived in this village, can tell you its entire history. Her brother, the late Arthur Weinert, was station agent from 1918 until his retirement in 1953, and Neustadt's railway service was obtained through the efforts of still another member of the Weinert family.

Probably the most famous person who ever travelled from this station was Canada's former Prime Minister John Diefenbaker. Neustadt was his birthplace, and it was the grandmother of Charlotte and Arthur Weinert who was midwife at his birth. The Diefenbaker family moved away from the village when young John was under five years of age, so his memories of that part of his life are probably few.

The Weinerts and Diefenbakers were among the early settlers of this German village, whose name when translated means "a new village." The first settler was David Winkler who came from Germany in 1855 and settled on the Meaux Creek. When grandfather John Weinert arrived, he too settled near the creek, and soon built the first tannery, also a boot and shoe factory.

The village grew steadily, but its future was hampered by lack of transportation and poor communication. Survival depended upon rail connections with larger Ontario centres. In 1876, John Weinert led a delegation which met with officials of the old Grand Trunk Railway in Toronto, and as a result, a line was completed two years later. The train came up from Palmerston, passed through Clifford, Harriston, Ayton, Neustadt, and continued on through Hanover, Chesley and Tara, then terminated at Allenford, about 15 miles west of Owen Sound.

Neustadt continued to grow, and with over 500 people in the village, they were able to support a flour mill, tannery, saw-mill and furniture factory, as well as being active in logging and farming.

With the new prosperity brought about by the arrival of the railway, four hotels were built, and each one flourished. There was the Queen's Hotel (every village had a Queen's Hotel), the American, the Commercial, and a Station Hotel. A horse-drawn livery coach met every train, and the most popular passengers were known as "drummers." They were salesmen from the city who travelled by train all around the countryside. Their samples and wares were packed in large black trunks – a far cry from modern merchandising. "Drummers" usually stayed at the Station Hotel, and used their rooms for display purposes. It was a festive occasion for rural shopkeepers, for while pondering, choosing and buying, they were treated to lusty cigars, lively conversation, and thirst quenchers commonly referred to as "a small libation."

In 1918 when Arthur Weinert became Neustadt's station agent, there were four daily passenger trains. Numerous freight trains were required for transporting logs, cattle, and furniture which had been built in the village. A great source of revenue came from the sale of Rock Elm logs which were sent to England and used in the construction of ships' masts.

Being a cousin to the station agent was a positive asset to Gordon Weinert when he attended public school. It was considered somewhat of a status symbol. Gordon was allowed to explore the ticket office and sit in the operator's chair in front of the bay window where he sent make-believe messages on the brass key. When young people in Neustadt reached the dating age, the railway station solved the dilemma of "Where shall we go tonight?". After stopping in at the general store and choosing two bottles of root beer, you and your lady friend walked the half mile to the station where you sat with your friends and watched the trains go by.

The builders of the Grand Trunk railway stations would have been proud indeed if they could have witnessed the amazing durability of their Neustadt station on April 5, 1929. The Meaux Creek which is normally passive in temperament, suddenly hit the village with torrential force, uprooting trees, flooding homes, and removing a sizeable section of the railway. When the flood subsided, the railway station was still snug and dry.

Many of the old branch lines of the early railways are neglected and see very little rail traffic today. Yet without them, the settlement and development of rural Ontario would never have occurred. On the line running through Neustadt passenger trains have been discontinued. The local way-freight is the only regular train today. Most of the railway stations are gone too. Palmerston still remains at the once busy junction, but the stations at

Clifford, Ayton and Tara are gone, and the pretty little turretted station at Chesley is boarded up. It's pleasing to see that Harriston's station was saved from the wrecker's hammer. It is now the recreation centre for senior citizens of the town who take immense pride in maintaining attractive lawns and gardens around the station, and keeping the building painted and in good repair.

You are aware from one quick glance at Neustadt's railway station that not a shadow of imagination graced its design. Despite this omission, this drab red frame building which served the community for over eighty years had that magical quality which manifested itself to almost everyone who knew the station – for them, it was the symbol of glamour, mystery and adventure.

Smithville T. H. & B Railway

The exquisite little railway station in Smithville with its Hansel and Gretel quality has the appearance of an illustration taken from the pages of a child's fairy-tale book. Its clean white clapboard walls are relieved by the fresh green of the shingled roof and trim around the windows and eavestroughing. A small circular waiting room is contained in the area below the turret, and bell-cast eaves projecting over the doorway, protect travellers against the elements. A tidy geometrical pattern is formed in green and white in a running band below the eaves of the turret, and is repeated below the gable over the baggage room.

A beautiful sunburst effect has been created in the small square glass panes above the narrow double-hung windows of the waiting room. A frosted sunburst is centered on the clear glass, and radiates to the finely etched detail in each frosted corner.

Daily passenger service is still in operation over this line of the Toronto Hamilton and Buffalo Railway. Passengers, wishing to alert the approaching train crews of their desire to board the train, have a unique signalling device. A green and white signal arm is attached to the top of a pole, and is connected to the ground by a cord. By pulling the rope the arm shoots up and can be seen well down the track.

This is possibly the most decorative station in the Niagara peninsula, and certainly the most whimsical ever built by the Toronto Hamilton and Buffalo Railway Company.

Kitchener CNR

When the Grand Trunk Railway built their Berlin station (now Kitchener) in 1897, a magnificent tower, complete with an elaborate spire rose high above the roof ridge. It was the only one of its kind in Ontario. When it was removed in 1967 because of structural deterioration, the station proper remained in its original state. However, the tower was missed by everyone in Kitchener. They looked upon it as the city's most outstanding landmark.

The predominant feature of the station is its series of graceful arches. The gracious entrance of the porte-cochère, sets a pleasant theme which continues in each set of windows and fan transom over the front entrance. Wooden brackets supporting the eaves extend to an ornamental brick ledge which runs horizontally between each window. It was the engineering firm of Gzowski and Company who built the Berlin station. This same firm had constructed the Grand Trunk line running between Toronto and Windsor.

Berlin was a "wood up" station for the wood-burning locomotives in the early days of the railway. It was estimated that six or seven thousand cords of hardwood were used at Berlin each year. The wood was placed in great piles along the station platform, and a steam saw cut the maple and beech logs into the right lengths for the locomotive tenders.

In the 1870s when wood became scarce and prices increased, peat was used as a fuel for a short time. Railway shops in Stratford began converting locomotives and in 1873 the first coal-burning engine was put into use. These early locomotives were lubricated with sheep tallow which the fireman carried in a pot. The nickname "The Tallow Pot" was soon given to him.

The first train came into Berlin on May 14, 1856, and by July there were four daily passenger trains – two from Toronto and two from Stratford. The average travelling time from Toronto to Berlin was three and a quarter hours, which included stops at Weston, Malton, Brampton, Georgetown, Acton, Rockwood, Guelph and Schantz.

Excursion trains were popular in the early days of the railway. The Grand Trunk Railway frequently ran these special day trips from Toronto or Niagara Falls to Berlin for a day's enjoyment in the town park.

Before a railway line was built up to Elmira in 1872, a stage-coach service operated between Elmira and Berlin. Long before daylight the stage would collect the mail, then stop in at the villages of Floradale, Yatton, Glenallen and Elmira. Before the arrival of the early morning train he would have his coachful of travellers at the Berlin station. The return trip was made in the evening after the arrival of the last train.

Train time was a busy time at the station. Behind the building, livery wagons lined up waiting to take passengers to the hotels, and a small horsedrawn streetcar also met the trains. These vehicles were able to cope with the snow by replacing their wheels with sleigh runners in winter.

In 1875 the Grand Trunk ran a line between Galt and Elmira, passing through Kitchener. Because of the European element in the area, the train became known as "The Dutch Mail." It was a popular line and made money for the railway despite its unorthodox habits and standards. The light rails used on the line limited the size of locomotives and the speed at which they could travel safely. Consequently the locomotives which shuttled back and forth along the line were usually small ones which had already seen many years of service and weren't built for speed.

Where the tracks passed through Blair and Doon, the flooding Speed River frequently made travelling precarious. Trains approaching the southern terminus in Galt, had to pass down George Street, a quiet residential street. Residents never ceased to fret at the sight of a smoking locomotive virtually brushing past their front porches. To make its northbound trip from Galt, the locomotive had to be turned about on a hand-operated turntable.

Train schedules weren't of essence to crews of the "Dutch Mail." If the ball game looked exciting in the park at Galt, the train would make an unscheduled stop. Passengers knew that they could be picked up at any point along the 25 mile track. They said it wasn't uncommon for the engineer to stop his train, get out and talk to a farmer about his crop. Tension and tranquillizers were unknown to that breed of men!

When the days of the old "Dutch Mail" came to an end, the romance of the railway seemed to depart with it. The old

Port Hope CNR

"Roustabout" is just a memory in the minds of a handful of old railroaders. Passenger service to Elmira has been discontinued for several years. Just the local way-freight is the only traffic along that hundred-year-old line. All that remains today to remind us of the early days of the railway in Berlin is the handsome red brick station in Kitchener.

A challenging new sphere opened up for many architects with the arrival of the railway! Stations were needed every few miles along the entire length of the line wherever the train stopped, and without examples of station architecture for reference, there was an opportunity for imagination and self-expression.

Frequently attempts were made to match the design of the station with the character of the town. The handsome cut-stone station built in 1856 by Grand Trunk Railway for Port Hope certainly complimented the dignity of this charming old lakeport town. The detail in the transoms and matching arched windows, and the beautifully balanced facade, illustrate the artistic skill used in the design of this station.

At one time Port Hope had three railways entering the town. Possibly the most picturesque was one called The Port Hope, Lindsay and Beaverton Railway. It was typical of the many small railways which flourished briefly before being absorbed by larger, more prosperous companies. This line opened on December 30, 1857 and meandered through farming communities on its way north. Its main purpose was to establish overland passage for the shipment of lumber from the Haliburton forests. Although the tracks have been gone for many years, the original station of this early company still exists and is used by the Ontario Department of Highways.

An aerial view of Port Hope shows several abandoned right-of-ways; one which had been the line for the Midland Railway and another running close to the lake built by Grand Trunk.

CN's Port Hope station has been closed for passenger service since 1970. Fortunately the building has been carefully preserved.

The Don Station

Time seems to have become suspended when you enter the waiting room of the little red Don station. Although a train hasn't stopped in front of the platform since the 1960s, everything about the station seems to be in readiness.

The station agent's cap hanging on a nail on the wall of his office seems to indicate that he's probably just out in the baggage room sorting parcels. The red lantern he will swing to flag down the train stands near the doorway along with the wooden hoop holding its orders for the train's crew. Although the Don station was taken from its original location and moved to the pioneer village at Todmorden Mills in 1968, none of its character has been lost.

It was built on the banks of the Don River beneath the Queen Street bridge back in 1899, and for people living in Toronto's east end it was a popular station. At least fifty trains passed by each day.

Although the station is a few miles north of its original site, the railway tracks and the same winding river can still be seen from the platform. Each time the engineer on a passing train blows his whistle at the crossing, it sounds almost like a salute to the old Don station.

When the station was built, railway architects were very keen about turrets and towers. The plain appearance of a wooden station instantly vanished when a turret was added. Its usual construction was a round shingled compartment with three windows facing the tracks. Above it rose a conical roof topped with a finial. Occasionally a weather vane replaced the finial, but it was not a common feature in Canadian railway stations.

Inside the office a wooden staircase led up to the turret room, and it was here the telegrapher sat all day in front of his key. His ability to decipher the messages of dots and dashes never ceased to amaze generations of travellers.

The decor of the Don's waiting room is similar to other small stations built in that era. It was dominated by the black pot-bellied stove. These old stoves were made by McClary Stove Company especially for the railways, and embossed on the coal door was a picture of a locomotive or a caboose. These stoves have become treasured by antique collectors.

Bolted to the wall of the waiting room is the framed copy of the company's tariff regulations, as well as the strongly worded advice to "Young Women Travelling Alone." There are also the travel posters showing steamships bound for foreign lands. After reading these posters, a train passenger whose ticket was stamped with Whitby or perhaps Manila Junction would probably feel a bit restless.

Although these small stations usually didn't witness the type of high drama commonplace at union stations, still they were regarded as the hub of social life. Little knots of people could always be seen watching the trains go by, or passing the time of day with the station agent.

Occasionally an unusual event would occur at the station, and it would be recorded in the local paper. During the 1920s there was a rash of break-ins at rural stations. One imaginative and resourceful station agent was determined to outwit the thieves. From the door and window he fastened a rope to the telephone receiver, so that the sudden movement would jar the receiver off the cradle. The night operator in the telephone office was advised of this plan, and was instructed to call the police if the railway station's telephone line should open during the night. (This was before the days of the dial telephone.) It finally occurred, and two startled thieves were immediately caught by the police. The drama did not end there unfortunately. The agent had installed an electrical device above the doorway which would flash if the door were opened. Not only did it flash, it short-circuited and flames threatened to destroy the building. Fortunately the fire engines arrived before too much damage took place. In a court hearing, ten merit marks were awarded to the station agent, but it was recommended that he leave electrical inventions to the experts.

That type of drama doesn't enter into the present life of the Don station. It now resides as part of the restored settlement, Todmorden Mills, where homes of two early settlers have been furnished in an authentic manner of the early 1800s, and a well-preserved brick mill stands beside the Don River. A finer location could not have been chosen for the retirement of the old Don railway station.

Brantford T.H. & B. Railway

Most railway stations have their own individual character. This is immediately apparent when you study the appearance of the Brantford station of the Toronto, Hamilton and Buffalo Railway. It has always imparted an air of cultured elegance.

The harmonious blending of cutstone, dark woodwork contrasting with the bricks of several warm shades, has created this effect. A pleasing pattern in the brick work was achieved by the use of three muted colours. A series of heavy wooden ornamental brackets supporting the eaves accentuate the artistic pattern of the brickwork. The dark stain applied to the doorway, brackets, and gables ornamentation provides an enriching contrast with the light tones of the brick and stones.

The Brantford station is an example of the variety in design used by the architects and engineers of the T.H. & B. Railway. Their original head office and station in Hamilton was a great red-brick rambling building, with all sorts of Victorian-style ornamentation. At the opposite end of the scale is the amusing little frame station in Smithville, looking like an illustration from Hansel and Gretel. The Brantford station has no resemblance to the other two. Each station built by the T.H. & B. showed originality in design, and demonstrated the enjoyment the architects took in this new field of construction.

The line on which the Brantford station stands, was built in 1895, supplying transportation between Hamilton and Waterford (about 50 miles southwest of Hamilton). It passed through Aberdeen, Summit, Jerseyville, Cainsville, Brantford, Scotland and terminated in Waterford. The decline in passenger revenue due to proper highways and the popularity of automobiles, forced the railway to discontinue rail travel of this line after sixty-five years' service.

Shortly after the Brantford railway station was closed, a group of businessmen who knew the station, and for whom it held many nostalgic memories, leased and converted the building into an attractive restaurant.

From the rail side of the station, few changes are apparent. Curtains on the windows are the only indication that it is no longer a railway station. An old-fashioned dining car stands on a piece of track at the rear of the station, adding atmosphere to the restaurant. Diners in this converted station experience additional atmosphere when a passing freight train sets off waves of vibrations causing silver and crystal to jingle their silvery tune.

During the 1800s every new railway was soon given a nickname. Underpaid, irate employees, or competitors usually made the choice. The names were not complimentary, but were accepted in good humour. The Toronto, Hamilton and Buffalo Railway became known as "To Hell and Back." By taking the first initial of each name in the title, imaginative monikers resulted. The Lake Erie and Northern which also ran in to Brantford was given the nickname "Late Every Night." The Algoma Central and Hudson Bay is still referred to as "All Curves Hills and Bumps." Discontent obviously affected the choice for the Brockville, Westport and Sault Ste. Marie Railway, when it became known as "Bad Wages, Seldom See Money." Probably the most unflattering title was given to the Port Arthur, Duluth and Western Railway, nicknamed "Poverty, Agony, Distress and Want."

Every phase of railroading had nicknames. There were "milk" trains, a name given to locals which stopped at every flag station. The "Roustabout" was a way-freight; there was a "Moonlight", "the crack train", and the unforgettable "Newfie Bullet" which had a permanent slow running order of 10 miles per hour.

Engineers on the trains were called "the hog" or "old eagle eye." Firemen, during the steam era, used sheep tallow to lubricate the engine, and became known as "the tallow pots." The conductor is still called "the Connie", and the brakeman is "the shack." Every train passenger will also remember the "wheel knocker" who appeared at each station, and walked the full length of the standing train, tapping each wheel with his hammer.

Probably no other piece of rolling stock has been given more nicknames than the caboose. Crews usually refer to it as "the van," but it is also known as the "crummy," the "dog house," or the "cripple's home." Anyone who has ever ridden in the old wooden cabooses which are disappearing from the railways, can understand the choice of the last name given. When retired railway men get together for a chat about the old days, they refer to it as "stirring up the cinders and black smoke."

Brantford also has a nickname. Proud residents refer to it as "The Telephone City," to honour the illustrious Alexander Graham Bell who lived in Brantford at the time of his discovery of the telephone in 1874. The original name given in 1827 was Brant's Ford. The present city was built on the site chosen by Joseph Brant and his Six Nations Indians for their headquarters.

For railway enthusiasts, Brantford has several charms. Not only has it the distinction of having been the centre where the first sleeping car was designed and built in 1860, it also has two outstandingly beautiful railway stations.

Guelph CNR

Great booms from the firing of cannon, interspersed with the shrill music of a brass band – flags lining the station platform – and cheering crowds – that's how they welcomed the first passenger train when the Grand Trunk Railway opened its line into Guelph on January 30, 1856.

A year later, the Great Western Railway opened a branch line between Galt and Guelph. An incident which occurred on the arrival of that first passenger train, was described in the Guelph Weekly Advertiser: "The only accident of the day was when a cow upset a pailful of milk which a dairy woman was engaged in drawing from her, when the engine snorted."

The trains of these two companies presented a colourful sight as they jogged around the countryside. The Great Western coaches were painted canary yellow with green trimming around the windows and doors. A lighter shade of yellow was chosen by Grand Trunk with window sash and frames painted brown.

The present CN station was built by the Grand Trunk Railway in 1911 to replace their original stone station, and the frame one used by Great Western Railway. It's an elaborate building combining Gothic features with an impressive Italianate tower. Mixing the various styles in one building never seemed to disturb railway architects.

When you approach the Guelph station today and stand within the area of the beautifully arched porte-cochère, you become aware of the graciousness so often associated with early railways.

Brantford CN

Aristocratic! No other word could possibly describe as well Brantford's CN station which was built by the old Grand Trunk Railway circa 1904.

The tall brick tower is, of course, the dominant feature. It arouses curiosity and like the towers in old European castles, adds an aura of mystery. After a light snowfall, the curved tiles of the roof stand out in a most startling manner, the white snow captured in each ridge, contrasting against the red tile, to produce a lovely effect. An amusing little tiled cupola projects from the roof, forming a protection over the bay-windowed signal office, in front of which can always be seen the old style green freight carts.

A ladies' waiting room occupies the east end of the station, and rising over it is the handsome red-tiled conical roof with four sets of windows running in ribbon fashion beneath it. These windows illuminate the high domed tile ceiling of the waiting room.

Travellers are still impressed by the porte-cochère with its graceful arches. In the days of horsedrawn coaches, it must have been a grand sensation when the equipage drew up to this regal entrance.

An elegant theme prevails even to the smallest detail throughout the interior of the station. Exquisite chandeliers with acorn-shaped globes enhance the ladies' waiting room. Sets of startling white pilasters rise from red bases, and above them are classic mouldings and enrichments. Total graciousness was achieved by the skillful blending of each artistic detail.

On January 13, 1854, Brantford celebrated its introduction to the railway when the Buffalo and Goderich Railway completed a line into the town. The *Brantford Expositor* reported that about 12,000 people gathered at the station despite the foul weather. A procession led by the Philharmonic Band paraded through the streets and arrived at the station at 2 o'clock to welcome the arrival of the first train. There were great bursts of cannon and cheers from the crowds when the first puff of smoke announced the approach of the locomotive. Following a lavish banquet, fireworks and a grand ball continued the celebrations which carried on until dawn.

The novelty of having a railway infected advertising copywriters and manufacturers who attached the name "railway" to almost any new product. Ads were run for "railway suspenders," "railway cook stoves," "railway salve," and "Railway Tonic for Pale Ladies."

Despite its exuberant welcome, the railway in Brantford was a losing proposition right from the beginning and by 1858 trains stopped running. In 1860, the line was taken over by the Grand Trunk Railway which ran it successfully until its amalgamation with the Canadian National Railway in 1923.

The most prestigious piece of rolling stock ever built in the Brantford shops of the Buffalo and Lake Huron Railway was a forty-foot sleeping car. It was built for the comfort of Edward Prince of Wales, son of Queen Victoria, who was touring Upper Canada in 1860. Thomas Burnley of Brantford had won the honour to build this unique coach when his design was accepted by the Governor General.

Never before had such luxury been built into a railway coach! Thick rugs carpeted the floor, and rich silk curtains draped each window. There were tapestried chairs and lounges, and built-in sleeping bunks. This was the first sleeper ever built. The exterior was painted a royal blue, and the Royal Coat of Arms was emblazoned on the side of the coach.

Unfortunately for Thomas Burnley, he neglected to have his sleeping car patented. If this detail had not been overlooked, we might all have travelled in "Burnleys" instead of Pullman cars.

It is gratifying to see that not a sign of decay or neglect is allowed to mar the CN station at Brantford. Flags fly on tall standards, surrounded by colourful flowerbeds, and well-kept lawns. Passenger trains from Toronto, bound for Windsor are frequent, and long freight trains rumble by, day and night.

Kincardine

When the Wellington, Grey and Bruce Railway completed the line into Kincardine in 1874, they chose one of the prettiest spots on the shores of Lake Huron for the terminus of their railway. At the mouth of the Penetangore River a wide stretch of pure white beach extends to the south, and it was along this tract that the line came to an end and the station was built.

If you stand on the front platform you look out over Lake Huron, and from the rear door of the handsome buff-brick station with its black slate roof you are just a few yards from the pretty little inner harbour of Kincardine. It's a scene of indescribable beauty with sailboats bobbing at their moorings or heading out the channel for a day of sailing on the lake, and seagulls wheeling and crying overhead.

It was on December 29, 1874 that the Wellington, Grey and Bruce Railway officially opened this line and the Kincardine station. The line originated in Guelph, then ran in a northwesterly direction through Fergus and Elora, on to Palmerston, Listowel, Brussels, Wingham, and Lucknow, and finally in to Kincardine. Up until that time, the village frequently suffered total isolation during the winter months from fierce storms which roared in off Lake Huron.

The Great Western Railway leased and operated the Kincardine line until the time of the amalgamation with the Grand Trunk Railway in 1882, and it in turn became amalgamated with the Canadian National Railway in 1923.

The first station built on the beach by the Wellington, Grey and Bruce was of frame construction and not built solidly enough to withstand the elements. The present station was built by the Grand Trunk Railway in 1903. Storms, raking pellets of ice, the relentless assault of blowing particles of sand, combined with the reflection of the sun's rays off the beach, have all contributed to the mellow patina of the warm, buff brick station. Only sturdy construction could survive in this location.

Just a few yards from where the tracks come to an abrupt end, families of spotted sandpipers build their nests in a partially concealed patch of reeds and grass. On the approach of a train, the frantic birds desert their nests and fly in frenzied fashion until convinced that their young are not in mortal danger. They persist in returning year after year despite the inconvenience caused by the railway.

Not only do birds respond to the appeal of Kincardine. It has also become the choice of many railroad men at retirement time. Mr. Matheson McGaw who became a mail clerk with the Grand Trunk in 1923 has memories of Kincardine station which go back to the turn of the century. Although he was just five or six years old at the time, he was fascinated by the railway, and made a habit of meeting the late afternoon train so that he could be on hand to greet his heroes – the train crew. He walked up through the village with the men and listened to their conversations which of course revolved around steam locomotives.

Mr. McGaw and his friends meet frequently to reminisce and share their wonderful old railway experiences. They recall the stormy January night when the train overran the end of the track and barely missed backing the coaches right into the harbour. On dark nights it was difficult to distinguish familiar landmarks, and on one occasion a passenger stepped off the train and walked into the harbour. Another mishap occurred when a motorist approaching the station from the road on the bridge, lost his sense of direction, and he, too, wound up in the harbour. Fortunately, lights in the area were improved and no further tragedies were recorded.

Winter storms made train travelling uncertain, and it was not uncommon for trains to be stranded in deep drifts for days at a time. Matheson McGaw remembers one particularly bad January storm when the mail courier was defeated by the wild gales while trying to cross the bridge over the Penetangore River. His horse and sleigh were blown against the side of the bridge and were rapidly disappearing beneath a wall of snow. It took two men to dig out the half frozen animal and lead him to safety.

A Mr. King was the first station agent Mr. McGaw could recall. He was there when the new station was built. Then came Mr. Chowen and finally Mr. Mathers, who was there when the station was closed.

A relief station master who frequently took the late shift had difficulty staying awake for the arrival of the early morning train. He solved his problem by chewing tobacco, and instead of using a spittoon, he aimed at a knothole in the floor, and

claimed he had never missed the target.

The Earl of Elgin and Kincardine, who was the Governor General of Canada from 1847 to 1854, must have been pleased indeed to have this delightful village, with its many scottish settlers, named in his honour.

It's difficult to determine which season of the year nature combines its best features to display the railway station. It could be in the fall when spectacular Lake Huron sunsets paint the sky, water and beach with glorious shades of scarlet streaked with violet and yellow. For a time, the station seems to absorb and glow with these gorgeous colours. Or it could be in the grip of winter when swirling blizzards assault the beach and snowdrifts curl over the railway tracks and station platform. Or perhaps the most appealing time would be on a soft summer evening when a quiet lapping can be heard as a gentle swell in the harbour rocks the anchored ships, and the roving beam from the white stone lighthouse catches the outline of their sails, before resting briefly on the Kincardine railway station on the beach.

Those early railway builders of the Wellington, Grey and Bruce would be saddened indeed if they saw this lovely railway station padlocked and boarded up. It is to be hoped that passenger service in Kincardine will be needed again, or that the railway station will be put to some worthy use.

Flag Stop in Rural Ontario

Gilford
Probably the most decorative flag station was at Gilford on Cook's Bay of Lake Simcoe. Four small gables on the roof are finished with overlapping rows of scalloped shingles. Windows on three sides of the station enabled passengers to see in both directions along the track without going outside. Gilford was a popular disembarking point for families heading for summer cottages. The line which passes through this village was Ontario's first railway, the Ontario, Simcoe and Huron, later known as the Northern Railway of Canada.

St. Mary's CNR

When travelling through southwestern Ontario towns and villages, you soon realize that railway architects in the 1800s must have embarked on each new assignment with enthusiasm and fresh imagination.

In almost every railway station, you find charming and truly unusual architectural details. For example, the brackets for overhanging eaves seldom were merely functional, but ornamental with great variety in in design. A whole book could be written about windows used in the stations; stained glass was not unusual in railway stations built before the turn of the century.

One of the most charming examples of the Grand Trunk's ability to create the unusual, is found in the station at St. Mary's, Ontario. Every approach to the station is a pleasure to behold. Trains from the east must cross a high stone bridge spanning the Trout Creek. Passengers in summertime look down to the river where a flock of swans drift gracefully by beneath the bridge. Coming into St. Mary's from the west end, the train emerges from a thickly treed cut, and stops at the base of gentle rolling hills at the spot which Grand Trunk officials thought was most suitable for their railway station. The location was originally owned by the village butcher, a Mr. Bone. The railway cleared away his shop and various sheds, but retained and converted Mr. Bone's house into a dwelling for the section foreman.

It is difficult to describe the colour of the present brick station because the overall effect is one of a skilled blending of tones of gray with a subtle suggestion of a warm yellow. The black slate roof provides an effective contrast to the mellow cast of the brick walls. This station was built circa 1902, and still gives the impression that it will serve the railway solidly for many more years.

Very few people can remember the old frame railway station built by the Grand Trunk Railway in 1858 which served St. Mary's for half a century. Until the arrival of the railway, the village had been a quiet place with few changes taking place. However, when the Grand Trunk built its line from Stratford through St. Mary's and on to London and Windsor, the whole tempo of life changed. Hotels were needed, and magnificent homes reflected the new status of the village. In the early days of opulence, skilled Scottish masons built an opera house in St. Mary's, which is still standing, although not in use. It is an elaborate structure, which rose to about sixty feet to a castellated battlement. The opera house became famous for its performances of Uncle Tom's Cabin, and Ben Hur, when chariots drawn by live horses would dash across the stage.

While St. Mary's continued to emerge from its early quieter life, the railway station soon acquired a club-like atmosphere for farmers who brought in cattle and produce to be shipped. They sat on the shiney oak benches in the waiting room, smoking and exchanging news and views on politics. A good number of brass spittoons were placed near the benches for the convenience of tobacco chewers, and a pot-bellied stove in the centre of the room was usually covered in winter with damp woolen caps and leather mitts. Hissing kerosene lanterns gave off their unforgettable aroma, and were the sole source of illumination. The sensitivities of ladies were protected from the rougher elements of the station by a private waiting room. In a compact recessed area, they could wait in dignity for the arrival of the train.

One of St. Mary's historians, Mr. L. W. "Curly" Wilson remembers well the old Grand Trunk Station. For him, and all his boyhood friends, the station acted like a magnet. In the late 1800s it had a particular appeal for young lads on Sundays when all forms of entertainment were considered evil on the Sabbath, and even shoe polishing was forbidden. After Sunday school was over for the day, Mr. Wilson recalls how he and all his friends hurried down to the station to see the "crack" Chicago train come in. If you had 5 cents in your pocket, you could buy a Chicago newspaper from the train's newsie. This, of course, was taboo, and you felt deliciously sinful if you had the courage to buy one. Every word was absorbed with relish, and spicey items were shared with eager listeners.

The most exciting day at the railway station was Saturday, when drovers began arriving in town with herds of cattle, and the boys picked up sticks to prod the bawling animals into the pens. The drovers usually had about twenty-five head of cattle to contend with, and their arrival in the village must have presented quite a sight, as despite shouted threats, the herd was more concerned

with sampling tasty flowers than meeting train schedules.

Today when you stroll through St. Mary's shaded streets, while pausing to admire examples of elegant Victorian architecture, it's difficult to visualize the town as it was in those heady days before the arrival of the railway. Like so many other Ontario towns, its original name is not the one used today. "Little Falls" was the first name chosen by early settlers. To honour Bishop John Strachan, they changed it to Mary, the name of the bishop's daughter, and prefixed it with "Saint." Bishop Strachan was held in high regard in the 1800s for his contribution to education. Not only was he the first bishop of Toronto, he was also a brilliant teacher, and it was through his influence that the first grammar schools were established in Upper Canada and funds provided for the assistance of public schools in every district.

The role of the railway in St. Mary's has changed and is less demanding than in the early days. When the Canadian National Railways took over the Grand Trunk in 1923, the station and line became a part of their system. Even the station's function has changed. One small room has been set aside for passengers, and at the present time, a health spa occupies the rest of the building. Fortunately, the exterior has not been altered. It is still the handsome railway station which was built with such pride by the Grand Trunk Railway.

Flag Stop in Rural Ontario

Crombies
About 10 miles north of Orangeville on the old Toronto Grey and Bruce (now CPR) the community of Crombies had its minute station. The carpenters gave it a touch of beauty by creating an almost fluted effect in the vertical board-and-batten contained within the gables at each end of the roof.

At about one-thirty in the afternoon, a handful of people usually gathered at the station to see the "Steamship Express" train go through on her way to Owen Sound. This train was considered glamorous because its passengers would complete their trips by sailing out of the Owen Sound harbour, destined for Sault Ste. Marie.

When passenger service was discontinued on this line, the Crombies station was moved to the pioneer village at Shelburne. It sits on an old piece of track under the protection of a vintage caboose which was retired from service.

St. Mary's Junction

An abandoned railway station is indeed a depressing sight but nothing could create a more forlorn effect than a forsaken station where the entire community has vanished too. This is the existing condition at St. Mary's Junction, just a mile or so northeast of the town of St. Mary's.

When you see a station with its windows boarded up, and the door padlocked, you become aware of vague feelings of regret and guilt. Why did we retreat from such a comfortable manner of travelling in favour of the car and the choking fumes of the highway?

The Junction station never acquired the gay sophistication which prevailed in the town's depot, and yet it achieved a place in history through the presence of one of its employees. In 1863, none other than Thomas Alva Edison was the night operator when he was just sixteen years old.

The main function of St. Mary's Junction was to act as a switching point along the main line from Stratford. Trains destined for London, Chatham and Windsor could pass right through after stopping for water, while Sarnia trains had to stop at the switch. The tracks took a southwesterly route, passing through Lucan, Ailsa Craig, Parkhill, Thedford, Forest and Camlachie before arriving at the St. Clair River terminus.

If you have travelled over the old Grand Trunk route (now Canadian National Railway) between Kingston and Toronto, you will have observed a similarity in style between some Eastern Ontario stations and St. Mary's Junction

station. An English firm of engineers, headed by Brassey, Peto and Betts, who were already famous for their railway construction in Britain and Europe, held the contract for the construction of the Grand Trunk Railway between Montreal and Toronto. The designs which they introduced in this area became so popular that modified copies were made in Southern Ontario. Features of the cut-stone station at St. Mary's Junction are similar to those in stations which Brassey built in English villages along the lines of the old Grand Junction Railway and the London and Southampton Railway. When you compare the stations at Port Hope, Ontario, and St. Mary's Junction, you recognize the strong Brassey influence. Both buildings were constructed with durable cut-limestone, and have the same Gothic design in the arched windows and doors.

The Grand Trunk Railway also built a turntable and large limestone roundhouse at the Junction. Here, too, the Gothic influence is evident in the entrance ways for locomotives. This roundhouse could accommodate six locomotives at a time, and usually was a storage depot for the overflow from the Stratford repair shops about 12 miles down the line. The building served for almost eighty years, and was finally demolished in 1930. There were also various construction sheds and houses for 300 Irish navvies who worked and lived out at the Junction as well as several cattle pens. Shipping days with the animals bawling out their objections to being herded into the lattice-sided freight cars were sheer bedlam.

The company's own pumping station kept the water tank filled at the Junction. From a little creek, about a mile down the track, soft water was brought in to the wooden water tower for the use of the steam locomotives. Engineers in the steam era claimed that the properties of soft water were far superior for their steam locomotives than the more common hard water.

There's an eerie feeling when you go out to the Junction today. The scene is a quiet one compared with the older days – gone are the navvies. Old Mr. Kerr, the station agent, Johnnie Davis, the operator and Jimmy Perdue, the baggageman, are just memories for a few old timers like Mr. L. W. "Curly" Wilson of St. Mary's who can still clearly recall activities at St. Mary's Junction in the 1890s.

When you step inside the old station, a few moments are required to accustom the eyes to the darkness, and dusty shadows. Time is needed to reconstruct in your imagination, the events which took place more than one hundred years ago when Thomas Edison was the night operator. As a protective measure against the possibility of the operator falling asleep while on duty, a company rule stated that he must type out the code signal "six" every thirty minutes during his shift. Young Edison was resourceful even though he was barely seventeen at the time. He invented a device controlled by a crank which would transmit the "six" call, and persuaded the night watchman to turn the crank while he slept. This arrangement proceeded without a hitch until one night when a message was sent

Fenelon Falls CNR

to hold a train on the passing track at Stratford. For some reason, the train crews did not receive the message which Edison was to relay. Fortunately the engineers of the two trains saw each other in time to stop and avert a wreck. It was recorded that Edison put on his hat during the investigation and "ended his career with the Grand Trunk Railway."

It is satisfying to know that this lovely old station at St. Mary's Junction has been spared, at least for the present time, from the wrecker's hammer. Fields of wild flowers surround the station and have graciously concealed every trace of the reckless demolition of a glorious past.

The majority of railway stations rapidly acquire a quality of abject defeat once they are closed for passenger service. Roofs become patchy as the wind carries off loose shingles, and curls of paint rising on weathered boards add to the general depressing atmosphere.

Somehow, Fenelon Falls railway station has maintained its dignity in retirement. You get the impression that it anticipates an early summons to renew its intended role. At one time it was a busy station, hard-pressed to accommodate the crowds of holidayers who streamed off trains during the summer months, while year round, crews from long freight trains carrying lumber from the Haliburton forests could be seen at the station picking up train orders.

Fenelon Falls' introduction to the railway came in 1872 when the Toronto Nipissing Railway built its line through to Coboconk. It was one of those uncommon, narrow gauge railways, with tracks laid 3'6" apart. (Standard gauge is 4'8½".)

To celebrate the coming of the railway, the company officials ran a special train, gaily decorated with flowers and bunting, and the passengers travelled on open flat cars. However, there is no record of discontent or complaints filed against the company for the informality of the journey.

The Victoria Railway Company ran a track through Fenelon Falls in 1878 on its Lindsay to Haliburton line, a distance of 56 miles. In 1882, by amalgamation, the Toronto and Nipissing, and the Victoria Railway became a part of the Midland Railway of Canada which consolidated with the Grand Trunk Railway in 1893.

Residents of Fenelon Falls have an affectionate feeling for their little red railway station with its attractive arched windows and neat gable over the operator's window. There are still a few old-timers who recall arriving at the station as settlers.

There is confidence in the town that the station will eventually be re-opened. Meanwhile, traffic at the station is limited to casual visits from the way-freight, and occasionally, an excursion train-load of steam railway enthusiasts.

Palmerston

In 1870 when the Wellington, Grey and Bruce Railway Company announced its intention to build a Southern Extension from a point 44 miles west of Guelph, the company chose Lot 19 on Concession II in Wallace Township, Wellington County, as a site for a station. This unsettled site became the nucleus of a town which soon would become known as Palmerston. It was a reversal of the customary procedure. At that time rural communities vied with one another in attempting to woo railway officials to choose their town for the construction of tracks and a station.

When it became known that this important new railway division would be made up of train shops, a round house, car repair shops, and a turntable, people rapidly moved into the area, and by 1874 Palmerston was a full-fledged town with mills, hotels, and a busy main street.

Until the arrival of the diesel locomotives in 1958, it was estimated that 75 per cent of Palmerston's population was employed by the railway. Today, the round house is gone, as well as the repair shops and turntable. Passenger service was discontinued in the early 1970s, and along with the railway station, all that remains of that once busy area, is the black iron footbridge spanning the eight tracks, and the recreational club across from the station.

Despite the changes in Palmerston, visitors sense that it's still a railway town. Almost everyone you speak to has stories to tell about the old railway days. The town is still full of retired railway men living in the same old homes where life

and activities were once governed by railway schedules.

Charlie Leakey's background is typical of so many railway pensioners in Palmerston. His paternal and maternal grandparents had been employed by the Wellington, Grey and Bruce Railway, and his father and uncles had been engineers with the Grand Trunk Railway. His wife's family story is almost identical – all railway employees.

Back in 1921 Charlie earned 25 cents an hour in his first job with the Grand Trunk. From midnight until 8 A.M., six days a week, he hustled through the dark town, knocking at the doors of engineers to arouse them from their sleep two hours before their train time. After working in the car repair shop, then as a fireman, he finally realized his life-long ambition when he became an engineer.

The duties of today's firemen are a far cry from those of the steam era, when on the run between Owen Sound and Palmerston, a fireman would shovel forty tons of coal! Meals out of a tin lunch pail could be monotonous for train crews, but a good thick steak cooked on a shovel always enhanced dinner time. Charlie Leakey's method was to heat the coal shovel to almost white-hot temperature in the fire box, then quickly drop the meat on to it. The memory of that treat still brings a smile to his face.

The Leakeys still live in the same house on James Street where Charlie has spent his entire life. Railway tracks run behind the back yard, and the view from the kitchen and bedroom windows is the railway station and all the tracks. It must

have been an exciting place for a small boy to live.

When you talk to railway men in Palmerston, the first event they describe is the winter of '47. Leaves were barely off the trees when the snow arrived, and until spring of 1948 scarcely a day passed without a fresh snowfall. The record occurred when 32 inches fell in one night. Old photographs show locomotives and cars almost completely buried beneath snowdrifts, stranded along the branch lines. Charlie Leakey remembers starting out to Fergus with the plough and five locomotives in an attempt to open the line. It was seven days later before he was able to return to Palmerston. One of his photographs of that occasion shows a snowplough sitting on top of a telephone pole. From the tops of snow banks they actually looked down onto the roofs of the trains.

From Palmerston junction railway tracks radiated like the spokes of a wheel. There's the line to Owen Sound, and south to Stratford. Branch lines go to Durham, Kincardine, Port Elgin, Southampton, as well as the lines to Guelph and Toronto. Tracks in front of the station were usually filled with trains, and the dispatcher was always busy keeping the traffic moving, and the lines cleared. The long black iron bridge over the tracks was built essentially for the safety of school children, and it's still a popular place for them to stand and watch the action at the station.

Palmerston's railway station has seen many changes since that day in 1871 when the "Adam Brown", chief locomotive of

Unionville CNR

the Wellington, Grey and Bruce steamed up the tracks. The company was absorbed by the Great Western Railway in 1875, which in turn became amalgamated with the Grand Trunk Railway in 1882, and finally became a part of the Canadian National system in 1923.

Originally the station was a single story structure, but business became so brisk in 1876, that a second story was added to provide the required office space. Early photographs show the two-story station with two ornate towers, complete with a Palladian window on the front facade. Heavy overhanging eaves spread out from above the windows on the first floor, and an attractively curved roof covered the semi-circular area of the ladies' waiting room. Over the years, these embellishments have been torn down; just a portion of one tower remains. Traces of interesting detail illustrate the original gracious architectural design.

Old #81, a CN Mogul type steam locomotive, which ended its active career performing branch service out of Palmerston in the 1950s, stands on a separate piece of track just across from the station – a fitting memorial to an old Ontario railway town.

Unionville's railway station never needed pillars, porte-cochères or Palladian windows to make it one of the most popular stations in Ontario with photographers. As soon as the morning sun lights up the simple facade, photographers can be seen setting up their tripods. Artists have always been attracted to the station, and even television crews, who use it frequently when they need to film a typical small town railway station.

There is a hidden beauty to the station that appeals to architects and fine cabinet makers – not one nail was used in the original beams, which were perfectly pegged instead.

The tracks we see today in front of the station are standard gauge 4'8½" tracks, but when the Toronto and Nipissing Railway built the line, it was a narrow-gauge railway. Construction began in 1870, and the tracks ran through Unionville, Markham, Uxbridge, and proceeded north through Lindsay, Fenelon Falls, and finally terminated at Coboconk. This was about 150 miles short of their Lake Nipissing objective.

The grain elevator, just beyond the station, provided a lucrative source of revenue for the railway, and the Stivers, one of Unionville's original families, owned the business. They had been a part of the William Berczy settlement which arrived in Markham Township in June 1794.

On the first Saturday in June each year, former residents of Unionville return by train to attend the annual Festival. One of the highlights of the homecoming is the first glimpse of the old station which holds

such nostalgic memories for them. The great-great granddaughters of Ira White, a miller, who settled in the area in 1819, travel all the way from Vancouver for the event. Ira White was the great-great grandson of the famous Peregrine White who was born on the Mayflower.

After 104 years, the Unionville railway station is still serving the community. A commuter train takes the business men to their offices in Toronto each morning, and brings them back on the 5:20 in the evening.

Orangeville CPR

Occasionally a house or public building acquires an indefinable romantic quality. When you see the CPR station in Orangeville, you are aware of that unexplainable phenomenon, for the station brings to mind nostalgic memories of the Toronto, Grey and Bruce Railway, that narrow gauge line which arrived in the village in the spring of 1871. It was an unusual railway, and it called for a complementing railway station. A wooden finial rises from the peak of the quaint black conical roof. Beneath it is the completely circular waiting room with its attractive grouping of windows. An ornamental dormer window was placed over the bay window of the station's office and to its right was the baggage room. A station restaurant occupied a two-story building to the south, and a few yards past it was the frame bunkhouse for trainmen. Each building was painted in CPR's famous mixture, "railway red."

As Orangeville was a divisional point on the railway, it was a place of constant action, and waiting passengers were never bored if their train happened to be late. In the days of wood-burning locomotives, Orangeville was the second "wood-up" station after leaving Toronto. Steam locomotives took on water at the tall wooden tower, and filled their tenders with coal from the chutes. If a locomotive had to be turned around, it was rolled onto the hand-operated turntable. And when the traveller felt hungry, he sat up to the counter in the restaurant and ate the best apple pie ever baked in the Caledon Hills.

For the first ten years of the Toronto Grey and Bruce Railway, passengers, villagers (and cattle) were constantly startled by the appearance of "The Caledon," that two-headed Fairlie locomotive, sister of "The Shedden" on the Toronto and Nipissing Railway line. Her two enormous stacks belched out voluminous clouds of black smoke, and the engineer had to have the skill of a juggler to keep his eyes on both fireboxes, and steam pressure gauges. They called "The Caledon" a freak, and no one was sorry when she was scrapped in 1881.

Passengers who travelled over this line which ran between Toronto and Owen Sound, thought the route was spectacular at any time of the year. Due to the abundance of twists and turns in the line as it worked its way through the Caledon Hills, it was never a fast trip. Passing over the famous horse-shoe curve near Melville Junction was an experience one never forgot! Every train had to proceed with extreme caution at this dangerous curve, and it was a nightmare for an engineer pulling a long freight. Derailments were common occurrences. In 1932, the CPR lifted this section of the line much to the pleasure of every railwayman.

Wonderful stories are told about this area by retired engineers who travelled over the line during the steam era. When the first train of the Toronto Grey and Bruce Railway arrived in Shelburne, about 12 miles north of Orangeville, a barrel of oysters provided a celebration feast.

In 1875 an entire train was buried under snow for six weeks after record-breaking snowfalls piled drifts to the height of telephone poles. Even today it is not unusual for diesel locomotives to be defeated by snow in the Orangeville district. Every railwayman who has ever worked in this snow-belt, has painful memories of trying to clear the tracks in one of the many cuts along this line.

Mr. Herbert Stitt who retired from the CPR in 1962 was a fireman and engineer during the depression years in Orangeville. Some of his most colourful memories centre on the meals he cooked over the coals in the engine. The finest New Year's Eve dinner he ever tasted was one which was cooked in the caboose while the train was on its way to Owen Sound. It was a night when the thermometer had dropped to almost 30° below zero, and the train's headlight picked up great menacing snow drifts which threatened to bring them to a halt. Back in the caboose two fat chickens were roasting in the oven, and on top of the stove a Christmas pudding was steaming. On the stroke of midnight, the crew sat down to an unforgettable feast.

Mr. Stitt recalls another occasion when he had to work on Christmas day. It seemed like such a dismal way to celebrate the day, until the train stopped at a village, and an old couple were waiting to give hot turkey legs to the crew. Such was the affection which people felt for railway men who worked such long hours in the days of the steam locomotives.

Good food always helped firemen forget the drudgery of having to shovel six or seven tons of coal between Toronto and Owen Sound. They claimed that the finest baked potatoes they ever tasted

Petersburg CNR

were cooked around the boiler. The coal shovel was cleaned off at meal time and served as a frying pan. The engineer and fireman placed strips of bacon on it, and when they began to sputter, eggs would be dropped beside the bacon, along with slices of bread to be toasted. A pot of steaming coffee completed the meal.

During the steam era, four passenger trains stopped at Orangeville each day, as well as mixed trains from the Elora and Teeswater subdivisions. On October 30, 1970, the last scheduled passenger train left Orangeville.

Despite the diminished activity at the station, people of the town still have an affectionate feeling for the railway which brought prosperity to the community more than 100 years ago. They rather enjoy listening to the morning ritual of the way-freight train as it shunts box cars off the siding and on to the main line. Through the south side of town, the railway tracks wind past the back gardens, cross a creek, and finally reach the open country.

The train does a lot of whistling after it leaves the Orangeville station on its way through town, but no one objects. It's their last nostalgic link with a romantic era.

Ever since 1856 the little Petersburg station, built by the Grand Trunk Railway, has played an important and versatile role in this farming community.

It was more than just a place where you caught a train. It was a fine place to discuss crops with neighbours, or to catch up on the local gossip, and it was a pleasant place to while away a warm summer evening. The station agent, who seemed to be an authority on most subjects was always in his office, ready to share his knowledge. Yes, the station was a wonderful place to visit. It symbolized mystery and glamour for farmers whose chores left them no time to taste city life.

In the shelter of the station platform, one could relax on an oak bench and watch sleek passenger trains streaking through to Windsor. Just watching the local freights with their remarkable names was a popular pastime. You soon became acquainted with train crews of the "Mad Dog," or the "Long East," or the "Roustabout" – all local freights which made daily stops in Petersburg.

One of the "regulars" at the station was Theodore Dietrich from Ste. Agatha. Every day he could be seen wistfully observing engineers oiling and greasing the great old steam locomotives. Although he never became a railway engineer, Mr. Dietrich won local fame by designing, building and flying his own airplane in 1921.

When the CN closed the station in 1968, it was moved to the Pioneer Village in historic Doon. Oliver "Happy" Engel and his wife Martha, who had been Petersburg's station agents for more than twenty-five years, were invited to remain with the station and act as guides to the thousands of visitors who attend the village each year.

The interior of the station is the same as it was in 1856. On cool days a comforting fire still burns in the shiney pot-bellied stove. The same enticing travel posters are tacked on the waiting-room walls, and "Happy" Engel still sits at the operator's table in front of the bay window tapping out messages in Morse code on the brass key.

With a little bit of imagination, you can still detect traces of the smell of kerosene, coal smoke, and wicker suitcases – all of which made up that unique aroma of old rural stations.

North Toronto CPR

In 1915 when there was still a great amount of vacant land throughout north Toronto, but the trend in construction was to the north, the CPR built its new railway station on Yonge Street, just south of St. Clair Avenue. Its 140-foot tall clock tower immediately became a city landmark.

This new railway station, designed by the prominent Toronto architects Darling and Pearson, replaced a small frame station which stood on the opposite side of the street. It was completed in 1916, and formally opened at a civic reception in June. Crowds filled the station platform, and bands played a salute to the departure of the first train. It was an impressive ceremony, but not by the standards of similar affairs in the mid 1800s when railways were still a novelty.

When it was built, the North Toronto CPR station was the most elegant railway station ever constructed in the city. A thirty-five-foot high coffered ceiling covered the area used for ticket offices, waiting rooms, a newsstand and general offices. Throughout the building, walls were covered with rich marble in subtle tones of beige, brown and green, and forming the detail of walls and ceiling was a magnificent dentil cornice. Covering the floor in harmonizing shades of light brown was terrazzo in a basket-weave pattern.

Three high arched windows form the predominant feature of the facade. At each end, and between the windows were four beautifully carved medallions illustrating appropriate railway motifs. A dentil cornice repeats the theme of the interior of the station, and the irregular roof line is suggestive of a battlement.

Brick and limestone were used to face the building, while terracotta in tones to blend with the station, was used on the tower. The four dials of the clock were eight feet in height, but have been covered over for several years.

On September 28, 1930, when lack of passenger traffic did not warrant continued operations, the station was closed, but reopened for one day on the occasion of the visit of King George VI and Queen Elizabeth in 1939.

Ever since the railway was introduced to Toronto in 1853, it has been a railway-orientated city. Since 1900, there have been at least twenty-six railway stations, as well as those used along the old Belt Line. Many of the stations are still standing and in active use. Beginning in downtown Toronto there is the Union Station, in Parkdale there are two, and the same in West Toronto. There is the North Toronto CPR station, Weston, the Don, Danforth, Scarborough Junction, Riverdale, South Parkdale, Leaside, Oriole, Davenport, and the Metropolitan station in North Toronto, known as Stop 26. The Great Western station which stood at the foot of Yonge St. became a vegetable and fruit market, and was destroyed by fire in the 1920s.

The interior of the North Toronto CPR station is a far cry from its appearance in 1916. It is now used as a liquor store, and all the embellishments which contributed to the grandeur of the station have been concealed. Rubber tile now covers the terrazzo floor, and the magnificent ceiling and cornice are hidden from view by a dropped false ceiling. The original wooden benches built around the walls of the smoking room are virtually the only remaining identifying features.

Fortunately, few alterations are evident in the exterior of the station. There is high optimism held for the preservation of the North Toronto CPR railway station. In 1975 it was selected by the Ontario Heritage Act as a building possessing historical and architectural value, and designation was authorized by Toronto City Council in October 1975.

Parkdale CNR

When you board the Barrie commuter at Toronto Union Station, your train heads northwest, passing below the black iron bridges at Spadina Avenue, and Bathurst Street. It then swings to the right of Cabin D, the control tower, and almost before you have had time to scan the headlines of your newspaper, you have arrived at the Parkdale station. You are still in the very heart of the city, and yet less than one hundred years ago, Parkdale was an independent village bordering on the western outskirts of Toronto.

Enthusiastic advertising of that era, described Parkdale as one of the most pleasant suburbs of the city. Because of its proximity to Lake Ontario, it was regarded as a health resort with great restorative powers. It was a popular holiday spa for business men who couldn't take sufficient time to travel any great distance, and commuter trains ran between South Parkdale and Toronto for their convenience.

When Parkdale had just 785 inhabitants, they were described in the Parkdale Register of 1885 as "intelligent and progressive to a high degree, . . . the cultured elements of society being liberally represented." This was the time when great rivalry existed between the socialites of Rosedale and the élite of Parkdale!

In 1878 when Parkdale was striving to attain the status of a village, enumeration showed that there was a shortage of inhabitants. With the date of incorporation approaching, some solution had to be found to increase the population, and it was suggested that a delegation should approach a tribe of gypsies who were camping in the area. If they would consent to become residents, Parkdale would have the required population of 800 necessary to become a village. Nomads by nature, and rebellious about putting down roots or accepting systems, the gypsies' leader agreed without enthusiasm to accept resident status for his tribe, and with a gift of $5 he returned to the camp.

If air pollution had been considered a serious problem in the 1880s, pollution counters would have been kept busy. There were no less than five different railways running through Parkdale at that time, and of course soft coal was the fuel for the trains. There was the Grand Trunk Railway, and the Great Western coming in from Hamilton, as well as the old Northern, the narrow gauge Toronto Grey and Bruce, and the Credit Valley Railway.

When the Grand Trunk built their station in Parkdale in the 1880s, it was a time of great elegance in railway furnishings. Coaches were works of art! Their interiors were extravagantly finished in solid rich mahogany. Seats in the sleeping cars were upholstered in deep plush, with matching drapes on each window, and each section was divided off by handsome wooden pillars. Elegant fixtures hung from the ceilings, and floors were covered with thick floral carpets. It was estimated that the value of the silverware in a dining car would exceed $3,000.

Private cars were in great demand by company executives and these were more luxurious than first-class accommodation. Pullman built one of these "homes on wheels" with a full size pipe organ at one end! Today's style of travelling cannot begin to compare with the grandeur enjoyed by travellers in the late 19th century.

Parkdale's CN station is standing at the present time, but is due to be demolished in 1976. Its design is reminiscent of the days when railway carpenters took pride in their ability to create a touch of elegance to the exterior of the stations. The Parkdale station is the only one in Toronto where one can see the ornamental barge boards which were so popular in Victorian architecture. Although the faded ivory paint is peeling, the attractive design can still be seen around the gables at each end of the building, and in the peak above the roof over the operator's bay window.

A railway station which has been forgotten by a community is indeed a depressing sight. An abandoned station platform, an empty waiting room with a few ancient fly-specked travel posters on the wall, and the semaphore on the roof are just about all that remain of the handsome old red-frame station built for Parkdale by the Grand Trunk Railway in 1885.

Shelburne

The sod-turning ceremony for the Toronto Grey and Bruce Railway was considered an occasion auspicious enough for the presence of royalty. Queen Victoria who had become an ardent train enthusiast was delighted to have her third son, Prince Arthur, accept the invitation to participate in the inaugural ceremony. The affair took place in Weston on October 5, 1869, and the young prince placed the sod on a small hand-turned wheelbarrow which the popular furniture craftsmen, Jacques and Hay, had made for the occasion. A small Union Jack was imbedded in the sod.

Construction of the narrow-gauge railway proceeded well, meeting its first engineering challenge in the Caledon Hills at the continuation of the Niagara escarpment. It was here that the famous "Horseshoe Curve" scaled the troublesome grade. (It became "infamous" after several derailments, and was abandoned in 1932.)

Settlers in Shelburne (originally known as Jelly's Corners) contracted to clear the right-of-way for the railway, and the heavy work was done with the assistance of oxen. In June 1873 the 122-mile track was completed between Toronto and Owen Sound on Georgian Bay.

The completion of the line called for a great celebration in Shelburne, and the new railway station was chosen for the scene of festivities. When Engineer David Weeks brought "The Owen Sound" with its string of little passenger cars into town, a memorable feast had been prepared for the crew and railway officials. The celebration was so successful, that the train's schedule was overlooked on that occasion.

Near the station a grain elevator was built, as well as stock yards, a potato-storage shed, and later, a wooden water tank. The village soon became an active shipping centre for grain and cattle. Four passenger trains, made up of six coaches and a parlour car, stopped at the station each day. Engineers who drove passenger trains in those days, always referred to their duty as "taking out the varnished cars."

The railway brought a new source of income for settlers in the Shelburne area by creating a demand for wood. The station was a wood-up point on the Toronto Grey and Bruce until coal became the fuel for locomotives.

During fine weather, travelling the length of this railway was 7 hours and 40 minutes of sheer delight, but in the grip of winter, train crews never knew when they might arrive home again. In 1875 the snow fell for seventy straight days, burying an entire train for six weeks. The rotary snowplough hadn't been invented at that time, and it was manual snow shovelling which finally released the stranded train.

Mr. Herbert Stitt, CPR engineer who ran the way-freight train between Orangeville and Owen Sound in 1928, still shudders at the memory of his experiences when his train was defeated by drifts in the long deep cuts near Shelburne. The steady uphill climb of the track until it reached Dundalk, 12 miles north of Shelburne, added to the problems of winter travelling. Trains would back up, then charge the solid wall of snow, repeating the performance until an opening was finally achieved. Train crews labouring under this stress worked up prodigious appetites, and found it heartening to concentrate on the thick stew which would be simmering in the iron pot on the caboose stove.

The last regular steam train run through Shelburne was in 1956. It was the southbound passenger train from Owen Sound – #1225, one of the last steam locomotives built for the CPR. George Wilkes was the engineer, Albert Bolton was fireman, Harold McLean, conductor, Ken Hunt and H. Stockton were the trainmen. No celebration took place at the station on that occasion. People stood at the track side, waving rather wistfully as the train pulled away for the last time. The Klaxon horn of the diesel would soon replace the wonderful eerie sounds of the steam whistle. The long, lonesome wails which fanned out across the fields and echoed through the hills, would be gone forever.

All passenger service along this line came to an end on October 30, 1970 – 101 years after Prince Arthur of Connaught had turned the first sod for Ontario's second narrow-gauge railway, the Toronto Grey and Bruce.

Before Shelburne's railway station had time to fall into the hands of vandals, it was bought by a Toronto family who moved it 5 miles south of the town to their farmland. The old waiting room is now the living room, and the agent's office became the kitchen. They remodelled the express room and turned it into an

Collingwood CNR

attractive dining room. The former freight space was sectioned off into four bedrooms. To maintain the authentic station atmosphere, the exterior of the old station is still painted in the familiar "railway red."

Although the station has gone, and all that remains is an ancient frame shed, with a single curved track running past, Shelburne still calls itself a railway town. Twice each day bells ring at the level crossings, and the harsh whistle of the diesel train announces the arrival of the way-freight bound for Owen Sound, pulling its string of box cars with the red caboose tagging along at the end.

Early fur traders would have been astonished by the changes at their Hens and Chickens Harbour on Lake Huron in 1855. Their 94 mile portage route to Toronto was now spanned by railway tracks of the Ontario, Simcoe and Huron Railway Company, and their trains were shuttling back and forth between the two lake ports in less than four hours. Even the name of their harbour was changed to Collingwood – a name which was considered more appropriate for the terminus of Upper Canada's first railroad.

Collingwood had continuous passenger service for more than one hundred years, beginning on January 1, 1855. The station was a popular departure point for settlers planning new lives in Simcoe or Grey counties. Three stations preceded the present handsome red brick building which CN built in 1932.

The most colourful celebration in Collingwood's history occurred on Monday, September 10, 1860 on the occasion of the visit of Queen Victoria's son, Albert Edward, Prince of Wales. When the royal train pulled up to the station, it passed beneath a magnificent arcade of twelve floral arches which spanned the tracks. The young prince, wearing a white top hat and standing on the regally decorated open observation car beneath this lavish floral display, was an unforgettable spectacle for the thousands who had gathered to greet him at the station.

Queen Victoria had probably told the prince about her first train trip. The Master of the Horse, who had always supervised her trips, was disturbed by her reckless decision to travel by train from Paddington to Windsor in 1842. He spent anxious hours examining the locomotive, and the royal coachman insisted on riding with the engineer. He wore his customary livery, and before the end of the trip, his white wig had been set ablaze from the sparks, and his red coat was black. The Queen was thrilled with the ride and became a confirmed railway enthusiast.

When passenger service was discontinued to Collingwood in 1970, the city bought the railway station and converted it into a museum. Although visitors are no longer treated to a band concert which welcomed travellers in the summer months, the nostalgia of this historic railway centre is soon recaptured when tourists examine the fine collection of railway artifacts which have been preserved in the museum.

Ridgeway CN

Railroad maps of lines in Southern Ontario in the 1880s look like the work of an inexperienced spider attempting to weave his first web. Most of the names of those early lines are not familiar to us today. There was the Canada Southern, the Great Western, the Grand Trunk, the Buffalo and Lake Huron, the Hamilton and North Western, the Credit Valley, the Northern, the Toronto and Nipissing, the Midland, and the Toronto Grey and Bruce. Many of these lines still exist, but we know them now as either Canadian Pacific or Canadian National.

The Buffalo and Lake Huron Railway built its line in 1856, joining Fort Erie with Goderich on Lake Huron, and the line was taken over by the Grand Trunk Railway in 1875. One of the prettiest stations ever built on the line was in Ridgeway, west of Fort Erie.

This station could well qualify for a study in window design. On the west end of the building which contains the waiting room, the curved glass in the windows matches the contour of the building, and the windows are protected by the overhanging eaves of the conical roof. A rectangular fan transom was placed above the waiting room door, and on each side of the entrance, narrow sidelights are glazed in delicately tinted pink pebbled glass. Above the bay window of the operator's office, an ornate square turret rises beyond the roof ridge. A Palladian window was built on its front elevation, with complimenting oval windows on the east and west sides of the turret. To complete the artistic architectural details of this exceptionally lovely old station, we find at the east end, an attractive wooden marquee supported by an ornamental latticework frame.

Waiting for the arrival of the train at this station must have been a real pleasure for passengers, because the interior was as handsome as the exterior. Below the conical roof a magnificent spiral ceiling was created, and only the patience of a skilled carpenter could have produced the exquisite effect. Interesting wooden decorations were created around the windows, and could also be found in areas which would not generally be seen, a proof of the pride the artisans of those days took in their work.

The first station in Ridgeway was called Bertie, the name of the township, although at that time, the village itself was known as Point Abino. Ridgeway gained entry into the annals of Canadian history when the Fenians staged their raid in that area on June 1, 1866. A newspaper account of the event reported that "a company of vulgar, ignorant and wicked men called Fenians crossed the river at Fort Erie. They were armed and intended to make war." The enemy was routed by the Queen's Own Rifles and a cairn was erected to honour the bravery at the Battle of Ridgeway.

In 1913, Albert Yaeck, the station agent at the Ridgeway Grand Trunk station, was credited for saving the village when fire threatened to destroy it. When he realized that local fire-fighting equipment could not combat the blaze, Mr. Yaeck called for assistance from Fort Erie and Port Colborne. Steam locomotives pulling tenders filled with water quickly arrived at the scene, and after pumping ten thousand gallons of water on the blazing buildings the fire was extinguished.

Albert Yaeck's railway record was a symbol of the dedication of old-time railway employees. He began working as a freight clerk in 1903 at the Grand Trunk Station in Waterloo. On his own time he learned to be a skilled telegraph operator, and qualified to handle the job at Grand Trunk's station in Goderich. In 1910 he took over the duties at the Ridgeway station and was there until his retirement in 1952. A real love for their work must have been born right into railway men in Mr. Yaeck's era. He recalls working twelve-hour shifts, seven days a week at one time in his career.

Residents of Ridgeway used to have a choice of four passenger trains each day. The noon train was the favourite with the ladies of the village. It took them to Buffalo and brought them home in time for dinner. The only rail activity on the line today is the occasional way-freight train.

By 1976, the tracks will be all that's left as a reminder of the old Buffalo and Lake Huron Railway Company. However, it's gratifying to know that Ridgeway's lovely little station will continue to be a pleasing site. It is going to be moved down the tracks to Fort Erie where it will form an important part of a railway display, and will be in the select company of another Queen of her time – CN's famous steam locomotive, old #6218.

Galt CNR

The story behind the name of a railway station can provide hours of entertaining research and bring to vivid life the history of the community.

John Galt, in whose honour the city of Galt was named, was a popular Scottish novelist – a contemporary and close friend of Lord Byron. After studying law at Lincoln's Inn, he was commissioned to come to Canada in 1826 to act as secretary of the Canada Land Act.

Spurring colonization in the area between Lake Huron and Lake Erie was John Galt's main objective. In 1827 he founded Guelph, and at that time the township of Galt was named after him. When he returned to Scotland two years later, he was financially ruined due to unprofitable investments. However, his time spent in Upper Canada was not without literary reward. It was while he travelled in Canada that he garnered material for one of his most successful novels, *Laurie Todd*, a story describing the trials of a Scottish settler in Canada. John Galt did not, however, live long enough to see the continuation of his work taken over by the builders of the early railways in Ontario.

The Great Western was the first railway in Galt. It was a branch line they extended from Harrisburg in 1854. Three years later the line was continued to Guelph. By 1860 the Grand Trunk Railway had taken over the Galt division and made it possible for passengers to travel to Toronto and Montreal by their existing line at Guelph.

The Grand Trunk revived and rebuilt an unsuccessful branch line which the Great Western had built in 1853 and abandoned in 1856. It was always known as "The Dutch Mail" because the area it served was settled primarily by Europeans. The line ran through Blair and Doon and on to Kitchener, and track maintenance on "The Dutch Mail" was an overwhelming task in the spring when the Grand and Speed Rivers overflowed their banks. The Grand Trunk continued the line up through St. Jacobs, north of Kitchener, and on to Elmira. The completed line running between Galt and Elmira was now 25 miles long.

"The Dutch Mail" was a financial success for many years, despite the air of comedy which seemed a part of it. It was operated in a casual manner, without too much stress ever placed on punctuality. The locomotives used on the line were light in weight because of the light tracks, and all had seen many years of service on other lines. Each morning students rode "The Dutch Mail" from small villages to attend high school in Galt or Kitchener.

When the line was built, permission had been granted to run the tracks through Dickson Park in Galt and down George Street to the station. Residents on George Street were constantly nettled by the sight of "The Roustabout" puffing and belching vile black smoke as it moved within feet of their front porches. For its return trip to Elmira, the locomotive had to be turned about on a hand-operated turn-table. This operation always attracted an appreciative audience among the boys. During baseball season, it was not unusual to see "The Roustabout" pulling to a halt in order to watch an inning at the baseball diamond in Dickson Park.

Passengers travelling on "The Dutch Mail" were picked up at the little stone station on George Street which was converted into a home when the line was discontinued. Those wishing to transfer to the main Grand Trunk line in Galt were taken across the town by horsedrawn livery to the station on Concession Street. This station still stands, although not in use for passenger service. It was designed in the style so favoured by the Grand Trunk. The series of arched windows and doorways is divided by graceful brackets supporting the eaves. In a gable on the roof above the telegraph operator's windows is an attractive set of three small round-arched windows. The dark stain of the bracketed eaves provides a pleasing contrast with the tone of the light bricks.

By 1881 Galt had the service of still another railway. The Credit Valley Railway extended its main Toronto to St. Thomas line through the north end of Galt, but like so many other Ontario communities, Galt is now without railway passenger service.

John Galt would have been gratified indeed if he had known that the railways fulfilled his dream for the settlement of the wooded area between Lake Huron and Lake Erie. The stories of the early railway days in Galt probably would have contributed material for another novel.

Newmarket

The history of the Ontario, Simcoe and Huron Railway is so filled with the romance of Canadian railroading that a feeling of great pride still exists in towns which were built on that famous line. Constant rail traffic passing through Newmarket serves as a daily reminder of the town's involvement with that old railway back in 1853.

Five weeks after the first passenger train had made its initial run to Machell's Corners (now Aurora) the line was completed to Newmarket. On June 4, 1853, a work train had gone as far as the unfinished Timothy Street Creek bridge, and had to back all the way south to Toronto. Finally all obstacles were overcome, and on June 20th the first passenger train steamed into town. It was pulled by James Good's steam locomotive "The Toronto." It must have been a tremendously exciting experience to see that pioneer locomotive with its four great driving wheels and enormous black smoke stack. At the controls of the little black locomotive were the bewhiskered engineer and his fireman – both heroes of the day. A baggage-smoking car followed behind the wood tender, and then came the small, brightly painted yellow passenger coach.

Fine cabinet makers today would have been delighted by the choice of lumber used in the finishing of early wooden railway coaches. Even the names of the wood have a pleasing sound. There was Norway pine, white ash, cherrywood and chestnut – ornate by today's standards, but how much more romantic than stainless steel.

More than an acre of land was purchased in the town for the site of the first railway station. Records show that the cost for this piece of property on Huron Street was just $2. The first station served until 1889, when it was replaced with a larger station, built by the Grand Trunk Railway which had taken over the railway line in 1888. The present station was built in 1900.

In 1857 a booklet titled "A Key To Canada" advertised "The Railroad Inn" on Main Street in Newmarket. A stagecoach met the train and took passengers to the inn. Accommodation in first class hotels at that time could be had for $2 per day.

In 1899, Newmarket had a commuter service provided by the Toronto and York Radial Railway. Five trips a day were made in the beginning. The electric coach, which also carried freight, proceeded north from Toronto, passing through York Mills, Thornhill, Richmond Hill, Aurora, and terminated in Newmarket. In 1909 the line was extended to Sutton on Lake Simcoe.

Radial cars ran on a single track with switches placed at strategic spots to allow the passage of cars. In 1948 the entire operation was discontinued, but memories are still vivid among people who used the line. The cars were extremely heavy, and about the size of a railway coach. Passengers sat on slippery black leather seats which could be flipped over to face the direction of travel. These radial cars travelled at speeds up to 60 miles an hour, and had a distressing way of swaying and dipping. They held no appeal to travellers who were subject to motion sickness! Frequent blowing of the strident whistle added to the excitement of riding on the radials.

The first public transportation between Newmarket and Toronto was a stagecoach. Competition of the railway proved to be too great, and on June 25, 1853, the final horse-drawn trip was made. However, in July of that same year, a stagecoach service was initiated between Newmarket and Sutton which was not yet connected by railway.

Newmarket's grey, vertical board-and-batten station with its red doors, is still in use for passengers, and is a well-preserved building. Separate waiting rooms for ladies and gentlemen were a common feature in Grand Trunk Railway stations, but their total separation by the presence of the ticket office, as is seen in the Newmarket station, must surely be unique. Not even the same doorway could be used to enter these two waiting rooms. Perhaps the architect was influenced by the line in Rudyard Kipling's Ballad of East and West: "never the twain shall meet."

The original interior of the station was brilliantly varnished pine. Today, however, it is hidden by many coats of uninteresting grey paint. Light fixtures were suspended from unusual round wooden sunburst-shaped designs on the ceilings. Dentil ornamentation formed the pattern in the cornice of the ladies' waiting room.

The last remaining piece of furniture installed by the Grand Trunk Railway was a massive oak desk in the ticket office. The importance of fine detail in the

Grimsby CNR

design of old furniture is revealed in this desk, for on each drawer-pull a delicate pattern was shaped in relief design.

Great changes have taken place in Newmarket's transportation in the past 123 years. First the stagecoach – then the wood burning locomotives – the old radial cars – and now the sleek, streamlined CN Supercontinental. This sophisticated train still travels along the line built by the pioneer railway, The Ontario, Simcoe and Huron, always affectionately referred to as the "Oats, Straw and Hay Railway."

In 1882 when the Grand Trunk Railway began constructing stations along their newly acquired line running through the Niagara Peninsula, railway architects had become more venturesome. The conservative designs used during the 1850s and 1860s were practically shelved, and the new railway stations became more ornamental. Grimsby's handsome station is an example of the imaginative trend which developed in that era.

Turrets were a popular characteristic of Victorian homes, and railway architects were aware of the prestige they added to any building. The combination of both a conical and polygonal turret gracing one roof was unusual, and the effect was indeed pleasing in the Grimsby station.

An impression of great height was given to this single story station by the vertical board-and-batten construction, the tall sets of narrow windows, the elongated brackets supporting the eaves, and the steeply pitched planes of the roof. As in most stations, the turrets were purely ornamental.

At one time Grimsby could boast three railway stations. When the Great Western Railway Company constructed the first line in the area in 1855, they erected a frame station which still stands directly behind the present CN station. After Great Western was taken over by the Grand Trunk Railway in 1882, another station was built near the popular Grimsby beach area to accommodate the crowds who travelled there on special excursion trains. It was called the Grimsby Park Station, and was destroyed by fire many years ago.

When railway construction was at its peak in the middle and latter half of the 19th century, banks began issuing currency decorated with the railway theme. In 1859 a five-dollar bill issued by the Bank of Brantford had a drawing of a steam locomotive pulling a string of square coaches. The Colonial Bank of Canada in Toronto decorated their 1856 ten-dollar bill with the sketch of a quaint woodburning locomotive standing at a station platform. In 1905 the Sterling Bank of Canada had a similar scene on their five-dollar bill. These bills are now rare and are treasures sought after among railway enthusiasts and coin collectors.

A likeness of the Grimsby station never appeared on Canadian currency, but it has always been one of Southern Ontario's most photographed stations, admired by artists and photographers for its Victorian elegance.

Whitby

For more than fifty years before the Grand Trunk Railway was built through the town now known as Whitby, settlers had gradually been taking up land. However, development was slow until the energetic Peter Perry took up residence in 1836. Through his efforts the natural harbour was improved, and soon became an important shipping centre.

The community became known as Perry's Corners. Twenty years later it became incorporated as a town and the name was changed to Whitby after the seaport and market town in Yorkshire, England.

The coming of the Grand Trunk Railway in 1856 created a feverish time of land speculation and inflation which ended quite disappointingly for many investors. The town of Whitby, although it was the County Town, just did not become the anticipated metropolis.

In 1869 Whitby began building its own little railway, a short line which would go north to Port Perry, and hopefully, beyond. It was called the Whitby and Port Perry Railway Company. Construction got off to a royal start when Queen Victoria's son, Prince Arthur, turned the first sod at a colourful ceremony. Celebrations today seem quite insipid compared with those held in the early years of the railway. The entire town was decorated with floral arches, flags and banners. Even the royal train was resplendent in garlands of cedar. Among the guests at the reception were the Governor General and Sir John A. Macdonald. An estimated crowd of 6000 was assembled to hear the speeches and witness the ceremony. For a railway which would be less than 25 miles in length in the beginning, this was indeed a lavish celebration.

By 1877 the line had been completed to Lindsay, and was affectionately referred to as the "Nip and Tuck." The morning train was always filled with school children from the villages of Myrtle and Brooklin. Their favourite prank was to jump off the train at the bottom of the hill approaching Whitby, then race to the top, pick a handful of wild flowers, then wait for the train to catch up. This rural line was acquired by the Midland Railway of Canada before becoming a part of the Grand Trunk Railway, and is not in existence today.

Whitby's Grand Trunk Station was the scene of another royal celebration when Edward Albert, Prince of Wales, made a brief stop there on September 7, 1860 on his way to Toronto. On this occasion every home and business establishment was decorated and the main street resembled one long floral arch. The usual firing of cannon, and ringing of church bells welcomed the young prince when he stepped off the train. After a short ceremony at the station, the Prince unfortunately had to be whisked off to the harbour where the royal ship "The Kingston" was waiting to take him to Toronto, and as the railway station was more than a mile out of town, the decorations in his honour were never seen by the Prince.

Passenger service on the Grand Trunk Railway was opened at Whitby in October 1856 and was in effect until 1969.

The railway station which was built in 1901 was closed and slated for demolition. Members of the Whitby Art Association could, however, visualize the station serving as an attractive centre for their activities, and the decision was made to buy and move it to a site across the tracks from its original location.

The lovely old building seems to breathe Victorian splendour. Three hexagonal turrets rise above the roof ridge, and beneath them were the ladies' waiting room, a general waiting room and the ticket office. Above each double-hung window, and in the transom over the doorways are three rows of small leaded glass windows. Pillars, rising from brick piers form corners of the gracious porte-cochère. The original dark red finish has been retained on the exterior of this frame station.

The interior layout of the station is essentially unchanged. Broadloom rugs now cover the floor of the main waiting room, and tastefully chosen furniture has replaced the old varnished benches, transforming the area into an attractive reception room. A kitchen now occupies the ticket office, and the long freight shed with its high windows now serves as an art gallery. The excavated basement contains rooms for art classes.

It would be impractical to believe that every old railway station should be preserved. However, the old Grand Trunk station which is now the Whitby Art Centre, is a fine example of a practical use for a retired station.

Clinton

Two long forgotten railways turned Clinton from a mere crossroads settlement into a town. But today, all the busy railway sidings, cattle-ramps, leaky water towers and stations are gone, and the last passenger train passed through the town on October 31, 1970.

It was in June 1858 when Clinton saw its first train puffing into town on the newly completed line of the Buffalo and Lake Huron Railway. This was a direct route running between Buffalo and Goderich, passing through Fort Erie, Paris, Stratford, Dublin, Seaforth and Clinton, then terminating 12 miles to the west in Goderich on Lake Huron.

The villagers were ecstatic over the arrival of the railway, and set about with enthusiasm to build stockyards and a weigh scale for the shipment of their cattle. The economy of the entire community was boosted by the constant demand for fuel for the wood-burning locomotives and farmers were kept busy carting in great loads of logs to the station, all cut into four foot lengths. The wooden water tank which was erected just beyond the station, resembled an out-sized sieve. Water seeped through every faulty joint, and by mid-winter the tower was just one big spectacular icicle.

The Buffalo and Lake Huron Railway was absorbed in 1875 by the Grand Trunk Railway, which in turn, became a part of the CNR in 1923.

Clinton's second railway was brought into being by the determination of an Irish settler, Patrick Kelly, who owned a saw-mill and lumber business in Blyth, 10 miles north of Clinton. He operated a brisk business, but progress was hampered by inadequate transportation. After winning the financial support of the people in his area, he persuaded the London, Huron and Bruce Railway to build a line running between London and Wingham. It would pass through Exeter and Hensall, on to Clinton and Londesborough, Blyth, Belgrave, and terminate in Wingham, 38 miles north of Clinton. Before the railway was completed, it was absorbed by the Great Western Railway Company.

There was an almost carnival air about this little railway. Its passenger train became affectionately known as "The Butter and Egg Special" when it was noted that on Saturdays, nearly every passenger was carrying a basket of butter and eggs on his way to market in London. For sixty-five years this railway won its way into the hearts and imagination of everyone along the line. Trains travelled at a leisurely pace, stopping on demand to take on or let off its passengers. Time schedules were not taken seriously by passengers or train crews.

It was on one of these western Ontario rural railways that an engineer won the reputation for possessing a deeper love for his locomotive than for his wife. For years he regarded the locomotive as his personal property, which only he could operate. At the end of the day he eased it into the round-house where it stayed until his return. It was recorded that passenger service was suspended for two days when the engineer suffered an illness!

The final trip of the "Butter and Egg Special" was a solemn and even tearful occasion for many long-time passengers who felt that a vital part of their way of life was being taken away. It was on April 26, 1941 – a Saturday – and on the platform of Clinton's station, it looked as though half the town had turned out to see CN's train #603 being brought in for the last time by engineer William Rowell.

Never before had there been a more sentimental journey. At every station passengers waited to board the train for this last run. On the final departure from each station, men were seen raising their hats in respect for the departure of this faithful friend.

When the line was ultimately closed to all rail traffic, the tracks were removed. Today, very little evidence remains of this quaint, loveable old railway. Traces of the abandoned right-of-way can be spotted in the countryside, and in Blyth, the station now privately owned, still stands, looking as cocky as ever with its new coat of paint. The Wingham station also remains, although not in use.

Clinton's railway station, built by the old Grand Trunk, was demolished in 1974. It was originally of frame construction, but in later years suffered the indignity of an insul-brick facing. It had few refinements in design apart from rather attractive brackets supporting the eaves. However, the waiting-room benches were indeed unique. A high-backed horse-shoe shaped wooden unit provided seating accommodation for twelve people. The seating area was divided equally by attractively shaped wooden armrests. On the back of each division a pattern had been created by a

series of holes punched through the veneer. Decorative wrought-iron grill work protected the entrance to the ticket wicket, and gracefully turned wooden brackets supported the counter.

Anyone who has lived in a rural community knows that the affection for their railway station is not determined by its appearance but by a personal feeling which has gradually grown through the association of memories.

The pride in their railway station, as shown for almost a century by the people of Clinton, recalls a way of life which will never again be experienced.

Flag Stop in Rural Ontario

Hillsburgh

The historic Credit Valley Railway was the line which came in to Hillsburgh. The attractive frame station they built has been gone for many years, but the present little red building is more than adequate, as passenger trains no longer use this line, and freight trains are seldom seen now.

When this section of the railway was opened to traffic in 1879, villagers were filled with excitement when they heard that Sir John A. Macdonald would attend the opening ceremony. However, an incident occurred that day which never ceased to gall the ladies of the Temperance Union. It was after the acceptance of their offer to supply comfortable chairs for Sir John and his party's use at the ceremony, that the temperance ladies heard about his reliance on alcohol. One can only imagine their discomfort when they saw a mildly inebriated Prime Minister sprawled in one of their chairs! The more liberal-minded element in the village chuckled at the dismay of the ladies of the Temperance Union, and took great delight in repeating the story over the years.

Prescott

Monday, December 25, 1854 – not only was it Christmas Day, but there was a second reason for rejoicing: the first passenger train on the Bytown and Prescott Railway was making its historic maiden journey. Never before had Prescott experienced such a celebration!

This event promised to be the initial step toward the creation of a great railway centre at Prescott. Lumber from Hull could now be shipped by rail to Prescott, where it would be transported across the river to an adjoining railway and carried on to Boston for shipment to overseas markets.

When the Grand Trunk Railway came through Prescott in November 1855, the town became an important railway junction for passengers travelling to Bytown, which became known as Ottawa in 1856.

The Bytown & Prescott Railway was run with great enthusiasm and by 1856 four passenger trains operated every day (except Sunday), two in each direction. The early morning train carried the mail, and had precedence over all traffic along the line. The later train was referred to as the "Accommodation train."

Benjamin French, the company's first superintendent, attached to the timetable, a long list of rules for train crews. He stated that "the clock at the Superintendent's Office at Prescott is the Standard Time." This, of course, was long before Sir Sandford Fleming's plan for universal Standard Time was proposed.

The most unusual regulation set forth by Superintendent French stated that "Freight Conductors are required to ride on top of trains, where they can apply the Brakes when necessary, and see that their men do their duty." Although the rate of speed did not exceed 15 miles per hour, riding on top of a freight car must have been somewhat perilous – certainly not a place for a man with a poor sense of balance!

Engineers in 1855 had to submit weekly reports to the company, outlining the activity of the train, the number of miles covered and expenses incurred. These included the quantity of wood purchased for fuel, number of tenders of water consumed, and the purchase of sheep tallow, and whale oil. These early locomotives burned whale oil in the train's headlight. Tallow was the lubrication used for the pistons and other moving parts of the locomotives.

Financial problems plagued the Ottawa and Prescott Railway even before its completion. In fact, the last 3 miles of the line were built with wooden rails when the supply of iron rails was depleted. The company was sold in 1856, and in the following year it became known as the St. Lawrence and Ottawa Railway. Finally in 1884, it became a part of the Canadian Pacific Railway.

Prescott also has a romantic history in connection with transportation along the St. Lawrence River. Enormous log rafts destined for Montreal would be towed down the river from Kingston. At the point where the first set of rapids was encountered, just below Prescott, the rafts were set free from the lines of the tugboat, and left to be guided through the treacherous rapids by fearless rivermen.

A great number of these rivermen were from the Mohawk tribe living on St. Regis Island. After safely delivering a log raft, they returned to Prescott by train to await their next river trip. This train became well known to people living between Montreal and Brockville, and for more than 100 years, it was always referred to as "The Moccasin" because of its popularity with the Mohawk Indians. Early residents of Prescott recalled seeing the Indians camping along the riverbank, waiting to catch sight of the approaching log booms.

Prescott was also a stopping point for pleasure boats which plied between Montreal and Chicago during the summer months, and the Grand Trunk would operate connecting trains for these steamers. In the 1870s the Merchants Line offered an incredibly attractive nineteen-day journey at the cost of a mere $38 which included meals and cabin. Advertising folders for this remarkable excursion asked the reader, "Are you weary, sick, or needing a change or freedom from care? At the end of 19 days on board the Merchants Line, you will be happy, rested, healthy, full of energy and able to face the battles of life with the vigor of a Trojan." If you were still not convinced of the exceptional merits of this offer, the copywriter went on to say, "Gentle reader, imagine if you can, how you can get so much for $38 in any other way on this great continent."

Prescott also tasted the excitement of intrigue. Smugglers built a series of tunnels from the St. Lawrence to the basements of various buildings along the

Uxbridge CNR

main street. High on the list of priorities were chests of tea, and wool and cotton from England, and one of the most colourful smugglers, known as "One Eyed Putney," used to row across the river under the cover of darkness, bringing with him his load of contraband cargo.

"The Moccasin" and the famous "Silk Train" which featured so prominently in Prescott's railway history, have been almost forgotten. Gone too, are the river rafts and their Indian pilots. The last remaining tie with Prescott's early railway days is its picturesque old stone station build by the Grand Trunk Railway in 1856. Its series of curved arched windows and doorways, and the four brick chimneys were all familiar features of railway stations built by the famous English railway engineering firm of Brassey, Peto and Betts who constructed the line from Montreal to Toronto.

It's difficult to imagine a community more enthusiastic than Uxbridge over the arrival of the railway. In 1869 they had voted a bonus of $50,000 to the Toronto and Nipissing Railway for the project, and the dividends received in pleasure and profit proved the wisdom of their investment.

Before the railway had completed the entire line, the company occasionally put on short excursion trips for the enjoyment of the villagers. Box cars with benches around the outside were the mode of travel – informal, uncomfortable, but no one complained.

The exuberance of the formal opening of the Toronto and Nipissing Railway on September 14, 1871 has never been eclipsed in Uxbridge. It was reported in the Uxbridge Journal that the railway was "open with considerable eclat."

For the occasion every home and business building was decorated. Union Jacks hung from windows, while ribbons and brilliant bunting stretched across the main street from house to house. Garlands of evergreens decorated the station, and across the front hung a banner with the wording, "Onward to Fort Garry." Floral arches were erected, each bearing mottoes that illustrated the town's enthusiasm: "Space Conquered," "Who'd Have Thought It," "The Old Times Have Vanished," "Labor Omnia Vincit," and "Broad Gauge Principle But Narrow Gauge Railways For Us."

A special train arrived at noon, bearing Ontario Cabinet ministers, city aldermen, railway officials and more than 300 guests. Following a brief ceremony at the

station by the welcoming committee, a brass band led the procession to the drill hall where a "handsome repast" was served. Toasts were proposed, speeches given, and eventually the party returned to the waiting coaches.

For several years the Toronto and Nipissing ran excursions to Toronto during the summer months on open flat cars. These trips soon acquired the nickname "The Watermelon Excursion" when it was noted that nearly everyone brought home a watermelon.

The station even served as a one-time maternity ward when a Mrs. Brewster arrived by train, stepped into the station and promptly gave birth to a son. They named him John Nipissing Brewster.

Passenger service at the Uxbridge station was discontinued on January 31, 1962 and the station was boarded up. However, in 1975, it was repainted, and an attractive apartment was built in the ticket office and waiting room for the use of the track foreman and his family.

Oakville Radial Railway Station

Half the fun of attending Sunday school picnics in the early part of this century was the ride on the radial car. The cars were big, and seemed to rocket through the countryside at terrific speeds. Children raced up and down the aisle urging the motorman to continue the fun, while mothers nervously clutched the arms of the wicker seats.

There were several of these radial railways in Ontario, but by the 1930s, their popularity had waned. Today, all that remains to remind us of those exciting trips is a few stations which were converted to new uses.

To compete with the lake boats which brought great crowds of picnickers to Oakville every year, the Hamilton Radial Railway extended its line to the town in 1906. The cost of the fare was just 35 cents, and most people thought they got full value for their money.

After boarding the train at the Hamilton station on King Street, passengers had time to settle themselves before the first stop on the Burlington Beach Strip. The town of Burlington was the next stop, and from there, the tracks left the lakefront, passed through Bronte and Craney's Corners, rattled over the radial bridge spanning the Sixteen Mile Creek, and finally came to a halt at the. Oakville terminus. The red brick station with its strange tower, still sits at the corner of Randall and Thomas Streets and is used as an office for an architectural firm.

Plans had been made to continue this line to Port Credit where it would merge with an existing line which terminated at Toronto Sunnyside Beach, but the idea was abandoned when passenger revenue fell off, forcing the company to discontinue service to Oakville. The last train on the line was in 1926, and several years later the bridge was removed.

A former station still exists on the Burlington strip, and is readily identifiable despite the fact that it is now a house. It is a small green and white frame building backing onto the rusting tracks. Bracketed eaves and a bay window are the identifying features.

In other parts of Ontario, old radial stations can still be found. The lovely old two-story station on Sutton's main street is now the office of a real-estate company. Hanging on a wall in the reception room is a photograph of the building when it was the radial station.

Probably the most exciting trip on any radial was the journey on the Toronto and York Radial, commonly called "the metropolitan." After leaving the car barns south of St. Clair Avenue on Yonge Street, the radial proceeded at a sedate pace until it arrived at the city limits and faced the long Hogg's Hollow hill. The hill seemed to present a challenge to even the most conservative motormen. The car would approach the top of the hill with caution, then in a moment it was careening down into the valley, rattling over the Don River bridge, threatening to leave the tracks at any moment. The motorman clanged the bell with his heel, and blew frequent warning blasts on the horn. The southbound train would be waiting on Stop 31 siding, known as Cemetery Siding. No doubt, the motorman was timing the speed of the northbound car. Bond Lake stop was the most popular place along the radial line. All summer the grounds would be filled with Sunday school picnics from Toronto.

When the Honourable Mr. Adam Beck proposed a 105-mile radial railway in 1914, joining Toronto, Port Perry, Markham and Newmarket, one of his selling points was "safety." He spoke of the skilled engineers who were designing cars for speed and safety. For further assurance he added, "We don't want, and won't have any car, which, if it topples over the banks will fall to pieces and kill you all, but one which, if it does topple will just churn you up a bit."

Those who can still remember riding on the radials will recall the queasy feeling they always had when these cars rocked and swung from side to side. You felt just a bit breathless from tension at the end of your journey. Nothing in today's manner of transportation can quite compare with the thrill of riding on the old radial railway cars.

Claremont CPR

At mileboard 166.2 on the Canadian Pacific's Havelock subdivision, your train will stop if flagged at the Claremont station. Your first impression might be, "just another dreary railway-red station." However, it was regarded with pride by the village, and for the family of the station agent it offered lively entertainment.

Mr. Kenneth Dopking who lived in the station for almost twenty years while his father was Claremont's station agent, was the envy of many of his young friends. When freight trains sat on the siding waiting for clearance to proceed, Kenneth could usually persuade the train crew to let him climb up into the cab of the steam engine, where he marvelled at all the valves and huge fire-box. His supreme moment came one day when the engineer allowed him to pull the throttle, and actually drive the locomotive down the track to the first switch!

Life in the station was governed by train schedules. Breakfast would be finished before the arrival of #381 which was due at Claremont at 7:04 A.M. Sharp on the stroke of 12 o'clock noon, dinner had to be ready so that it wouldn't interfere with #383 which came in at 12:42 P.M. The entire day was punctuated by the arrivals and departures of passenger trains, and the thunder of a passing freight train acted as a conversation stopper for anyone visiting the Dopkings. Windows rattled, dishes and silver vibrated a metallic tune, and pictures hanging on the walls took on a new angle.

Competition was keen among station agents who strived for outstanding lawns and flower gardens. Claremont won the railway award on many occasions for the perfection of its shapely cedar hedge and colourful flowers bordering the lawns and the willow tree which cast lacey shadows against the frame station.

During the winter months, snow-ploughs are in constant use keeping open the line passing through Claremont. However, a paralyzing storm in 1959 brought rail traffic to a standstill. Passengers slept in the station that night. Wood stoves were used for heating and cooking after a power failure when the hydro wires came down. Telephone service was cut off too, and Claremont appeared to be totally isolated. However, the unexpected appearance of a beer truck, churning through snowdrifts which had defeated county snow-ploughs cheered the passengers up.

Mr. Herbert Stitt, retired CP engineer has a very special recollection of Claremont. His train had stopped in Pontypool to pick up train orders which he found hard to believe. The message read, "Be on lookout for elephant on tracks at Claremont." Stray cattle and deer were not unusual on the tracks, but who would expect to find an elephant? Apparently one had escaped while being unloaded from a circus train at Whitby, and when last seen was lumbering up the CPR tracks in a westerly direction.

An air of mystery veiled the identity of an itinerant worker many years ago in Claremont whose highway was the railroad. He was known simply as "John the Fan Cutter." After doing odd jobs at a farm, restlessness would soon urge him to move on. If he had been treated well at the farm, he would whittle an exquisite wooden fan, and present it on his departure before disappearing down the tracks, carrying his worldly belongings in a knotted bandana.

During the depression years, people like "John the Fan Cutter" were not uncommon in rural villages. At another station on Havelock subdivision, a homeless man made his winter home in the basement. A cultured man, he was an authority on every known religion, and was called "Bible Bill."

The company which built the railway line running through Claremont was another example of the small railway companies whose life time was so short in the late 1800s. In 1884, the Ontario and Quebec Railway Company constructed the line, and in the same year, it was purchased by the Canadian Pacific Railway company who have operated it since that time.

Barrie CNR

When the Ontario, Simcoe and Huron Railway surveyed the line between Toronto and Collingwood it was agreed that the railway would enter the village of Barrie on Lake Simcoe. However, when construction reached the area in October 1853, it was at Allandale, a mile south of Barrie, where the company decided to swing to the northwest on the continuation to Collingwood. After a great deal of bitterness, the line was continued into Barrie on June 21, 1865, and the town had a station of its own. Ultimately, Allandale was absorbed by Barrie.

Several years ago the old Barrie railway station was demolished, and since then the Allandale station (renamed Barrie) has served the entire community.

Financial difficulties plagued the railway throughout the construction period. It was not until 1861 that money was raised for track ballast and fencing along the line. The Ontario, Simcoe and Huron Railway represented the first major development in which settlers could invest. Ira White, a farmer and miller in Markham, was typical of these early investors. Although he would not personally benefit by the railway because its location was so far from his home, he believed that his purchase of railway shares demonstrated his confidence in the future of the country he had chosen.

In 1868 Allandale's station became the first to have a restaurant. It was built with the emphasis on graciousness. Fine paintings decorated the walls, and tables were spread with white linen and silver. A white picket fence surrounded colourful gardens and the well-kept lawn in front of the station.

The elegance of the station restaurant must have deteriorated over the years. Harriet Black, a seventeen-year-old Toronto girl tells in a letter her impressions of a train trip from Muskoka to the Allandale station in 1907.

"It was the dirtiest train car I ever got into. If you left the windows closed, you roasted and smothered. If you opened them you were buried in cinders in two minutes and had constantly to keep taking them out of your eyes. Then the awful smell of that horrid smoke. It is enough to make anyone sick. If I were an engineer I would put the engine at the back and shove the cars ahead so that the smoke would not bother the passengers. What is the use of all the men in the world if one cannot invent a decent clean engine that won't blow all its dirty smoke and cinders on to the cars? Oh! I wish I were a man! When we got to Allandale, the train stopped and all the passengers got off and rushed into the restaurant. There were hundreds of people and only four men to serve them, and only ten minutes to do it in. Consequently many people came away hungry. We at last got a plate of sandwiches and two cups of coffee which was too hot to drink. Before it had time to cool off, the gong rang for us to go back to the train. I burned my tongue trying to swallow a mouthful of coffee, then ran out onto the platform and jumped on the train just a few seconds before it started. The remainder of the ride home was uneventful but very dirty."

If Harriet were alive today, she would surely scoff at people who speak of the nostalgia of the romantic steam era!

It was the Grand Trunk Railway which built the last station at Allandale or Barrie as it is now called. It is a divisional point on the line and has considerable office space, an abandoned restaurant area, and a main building containing waiting rooms, a ticket office and baggage room.

The four Tuscan pillars forming an entrance to the central building are flanked by wide divided windows on each side. A ballustrade made up of five pillars creates an ornamental effect above these windows. Attractive brackets support the eaves of the main and second floors of each building.

Another handsome feature of the station construction is the semi-circular waiting room facing southeast. Above the red brick base is a set of six double-hung windows with an interesting geometrical pattern in the upper section. The final touch in the design of the waiting room area is an unusual and handsome coronet effect surrounding the circular roof.

When you wait for your train today at the old Allandale station, you look beyond the maze of tracks and railway cars to a view of Kempenfeldt Bay, a scene which brings to mind the days when, long before the coming of the railway, Indians used this same trail to carry their furs from Lake Huron to the village of York.

Fergus

Fergus, a Scottish farming community north of Guelph, had to wait until 1870 for its first railroad. Adam Fergusson had visited Canada in 1831 on behalf of the Highland Society of Scotland, and two years later, he and James Webster purchased seven thousand acres of land in Nichol township. By 1835, a sawmill, a grist mill and a school had been erected. Soon, the population of the area grew to sixteen hundred. All that was needed to complete Adam Fergusson's dream of a prosperous development was the presence of a railroad.

Another Scotsman, Adam Brown of Hamilton, obtained a railway charter to build a line from Guelph, up through Fergus, Elora, and terminating in Kincardine on Lake Huron. He called his railway The Wellington, Grey and Bruce, and construction began on June 20, 1867.

The sod-turning ceremony called for a holiday in the village and almost everyone took part in it. Mr. George D. Fergusson pushing a wheelbarrow, James Wilson with a pickaxe, and John Fraser with a shovel, headed up a grand parade. These men had contributed generously to the promotion of the railway, and it was felt that they should have the honour of carrying the tools which would be used to cut, turn and lift the first piece of sod. The Fergus Rifle Company and all the school children, followed by the adults, marched two-by-two behind the Fergus Brass Band to the spot chosen by Mr. W. Shanly, the chief surveyor. After prayers and scripture readings by the Reverend George MacDonnell, Mr. Adam Brown, president of the railway, cut the sod. The brass band struck up some appropriate music, and the crowds cheered as the sod was wheeled away in the specially built wheelbarrow. An enthusiastic celebration took place at the North American Hotel, and toasts were proposed to the success of Adam Brown's railway.

Early in the construction period, the company became plagued by financial difficulties. Fortunately the Great Western Railway, which ran into Guelph from Hamilton, saved the situation by an agreement to operate the road in connection with their own. They would supply the locomotives and rolling stock, and the Wellington, Grey and Bruce agreed to build the railroad, all the stations, freight sheds and water towers.

Construction was completed and the first passenger train pulled in to Fergus on September 13, 1870. This long-awaited event called for another holiday and celebration.

Villagers gathered at the station hours before the train was due to witness this scene of unparalleled gaiety. The newly built station was decorated with flags and bunting, and a magnificent floral arch spanned the tracks. The ladies of the village, all dressed in long sweeping skirts and their finest hats, had tables set up on the station platform, and were prepared to serve a great feast to the crowds. The locomotive pulling that first passenger train was appropriately named "The Adam Brown." Cheers went up as the train passed beneath the floral arch and came to a stop beside the station and a grand ball was held that night to complete the celebrations of that memorable day.

A week later, the Wellington, Grey and Bruce put on its first excursion. It was to be a day trip to Niagara Falls, at the cost of $1 per person. A notice was published that passengers were absolutely forbidden to ride on the roof of the coaches. The flat roofs of these early coaches were a tempting invitation for a bit of fun for the village lads. Some would even jump from roof to roof as the coaches were in motion!

After this excursion train left the village, it was to pick up five coach-loads of excursionists at the Elora station. An inexperienced switchman apparently turned the switch in the wrong direction, and sent the train slamming into the waiting coaches. There were no injuries, but a considerable amount of damage was done to the coaches. After a delay of several hours, the train finally set off again, and without further mishap arrived in Niagara. On the return trip a lighter locomotive was put on to replace the Adam Brown. This presented a problem each time the train approached a grade. The little locomotive eventually arrived back in Fergus at 4 A.M. The passengers took it all in good spirit.

Fergus got a second railroad in 1879 when the Credit Valley Railway ran in a branch line to Elora. A photograph of their station which is shown here is an example of how railway architecture was frequently influenced by the prevailing architecture of the area. The simple cottage style with a single gable over the entrance is seen everywhere in the Fergus area. This station disappeared in the early 1970s when passenger service was

Concord CNR

discontinued. CPR took over the operation of the Credit Valley Railway in 1883, and still runs a way-freight along this line. Its arrival is still welcomed by old-time residents of Fergus whose lives had been affected by the railways, and who have such colourful memories of the past.

Concord's colourful historic background gives this station a unique status in Canadian railway lore.

In October 1852, just a year after the commencement of construction of the Ontario Simcoe and Huron Railway, 14 miles of track had been laid, reaching the village of Concord. Plans were set in motion for a trial run on this line. For the occasion, a locomotive was purchased in Maine and shipped by sailing schooner across Lake Ontario to Toronto's harbour. They christened her "The Lady Elgin," in honour of the Countess of Elgin, wife of Canada's Governor General, who had turned the first sod for the railway in 1851. Tremendous crowds turned out to watch the departure of the train on this inaugural trip, and above their cheers could be heard the jubilant shrieks of the steam whistle.

The first train wreck recorded in Canadian history occurred near this station on Sunday, July 17, 1853. The victims were one cow, and a baggage car. One can sympathize with the consternation of a dairy herd when suddenly their serene pasture was defiled by a snorting, fire-breathing black object, propelled on eight wheels – the showers of sparks and belching clouds of black smoke must have resembled some half-crazed mythical monster. The unfortunate cow which was struck by the train caused the derailment of the third coach, which was totally demolished after rolling down an embankment, but "The Lady Elgin" survived the ordeal with dignity.

From 1855 to 1880, Mr. Duncan and his seven daughters ran the station. He had taught each girl to operate the telegrapher's key, so that he was free to attend to passenger traffic and freight shipments.

Barlow Cumberland is said to have designed the attractive vertical board-and-batten station. The simplicity of its style is enhanced by lovely detail in the arched windows and a handsome fan transom above the waiting-room doorway. The neat white gable and overhanging eaves are supported by delicately shaped wrought-iron brackets.

Although the station is not in use for passenger traffic today, a well-cared-for appearance has been maintained. One can only hope that it will be preserved for its architectural merit and historical significance.

Brampton CNR

If a man had once made a round trip from Brampton to Toronto by stagecoach in the early 1800s, no form of inducement could have persuaded him to travel that way again! The trip would have taken two bone-jarring days, and at least once during the journey, he would have been called upon to help push the coach through muddy bogs which had defeated the team of horses. Overland travelling had few charms in those days. It was a time of immense relief and an occasion for celebration when the Grand Trunk Railway opened its line through the village of Brampton on June 16, 1856.

This backwood community soon attained town status, and by 1879 had a second railway, when the Credit Valley Railway constructed its line from Toronto, through Brampton, and on to Orangeville.

The Grand Trunk Railway published a booklet in 1857, titled "A Key To Canada," which gave the names of all communities along its lines, as well as the names of stagecoaches which met trains and carried passengers to villages which were not on railroad lines. The booklet urged passengers to bear in mind that "No trains run, nor steamers start upon Sundays, and calculate time and cost, and regulate journey accordingly." Names of hotels and inns were included in the booklet, as well as their prevailing rates. To encourage travelling, assurance was given that "Nearly everywhere in Canada, hotel accommodation is provided, of some description or other; and no journey need ever be broken for fear of losing it altogether. In remote places a greater degree of comfort may be found than might be expected; but of course allowance will be made for absence of style and delicacy. We have often received greater hospitality and experienced a liberality in fare, a cleanliness in all essentials, and an economy in charge, that has made the recollection of a sojourn at a way-side house far more pleasing than that made at many houses of greater pretense."

Accommodation ranged in price from $2 per day for first class; $1 to $2 for intermediate; and just $1 for third class. Substantial meals were included in the tariff.

On the advent of the railways in Canada in the early 1850s, there were those who prophesied that the "iron horse" would be a failure, but they were now in the minority. Stephenson had successfully run his train "Locomotion" between Stockton and Darlington in England in 1825, and went on to convince the British parliament that a railroad should be constructed between Liverpool and Manchester. In a stormy parliamentary debate before the bill was passed, Lord Lefton declared that "Stephenson's locomotives would poison the air, kill the birds as they flew over them, destroy the preservation of pheasants, burn up the farms and homesteads near the lines; that oats and hay would be unsaleable because horses would become extinct; travelling on the highways would become impossible; country inns would be ruined; boilers would burst and kill hundreds of passengers." Despite Lord Lefton's gloomy predictions, railways flourished in England, and by the late 1830s settlers in Canada began clamouring for them.

The popularity and success of the railways in Canada is reflected in the imaginative and often majestic architecture of railway stations. The regal elegance of Brampton's Canadian National station forcefully substantiates this fact. From the porte-cochère on the east end of the building, and continuing with each window and doorway, the main design theme is one of graceful arches, their fluid lines softening the stern dignity of the station. Circular turrets flank a modified tower, and the pitch of the various planes of the roof suggest the influence of French chateau architecture.

Several warm shades of brick are blended to form a pleasing pattern throughout the building, and impart a mellowness to the appearance, while white wooden brackets spaced beneath the eaves at short intervals, add extra embellishment, while remaining functional.

For almost 120 years, Brampton has had continuous passenger service on the line built by the old Grand Trunk Railway (now CNR). Settlers in the early 1800s would have been filled with disbelief if they had been told that a commuter service would whisk passengers between Toronto and Brampton in just forty minutes.

Hamilton CNR

Ontario's final contribution to grandeur in railway station architecture came in 1930 with the building of Hamilton's Canadian National Railway station. From a distance, it could easily be mistaken for a magnificent art gallery or a court house, the great pillars symbolizing authority.

This was the fourth station to have been built in this same area; the first two constructed by the Great Western Railway, and the third by the Grand Trunk Railway. This last station was Gothic in design, with arched windows and ornamental "gingerbread" in the bargeboard of the gabled roof. It served Hamilton passengers from the 1880s until the new station was opened in 1930.

Good fortune, or planning, provided a great expanse of lawn at the front of the station, making the study and enjoyment of the building possible without extraneous distractions. On a simple frieze spanning the four fluted pillars, the engraved name "Canadian National Railways" stands between circular ornamental festoons. Fanlike acroterions grace the outer corners of the pediment, and at the peak of the gabled pediment stands an ornate anthemion.

Between the four pillars, vertical tablets in bas relief illustrate the transportation theme. The outer two show steam locomotives used by the CNR in the early days of the century. In the centre portion, a line of box cars is shown being filled with grain from the holds of a lake boat. The ornamental grill work, and the groups of windows below and above the stone tablets give the impression of frames around the tablets.

A public holiday was proclaimed on January 19, 1854 to mark Hamilton's entry to the railway era. The completion of the Great Western's railway line joining Hamilton, Niagara Falls and Windsor called for a tumultuous celebration. At that moment it became the longest railway in Canada. On that long-awaited occasion, no one was more jubilant than Sir Allan Napier MacNab who had been the driving force behind the building of the Great Western Railway. He was the first president of the railway, and was also actively engaged in politics. During the war of 1812 he had served in the navy and army, was decorated for outstanding bravery in the Rebellion of 1837, and his home, Dundurn Castle, is now Hamilton's museum. It was a blessing that he died before the Great Western Railway experienced grave financial problems, which brought about its amalgamation in 1882 with its former rival, the Grand Trunk Railway.

The Great Western had completed branch lines running from Harrisburg to Galt in 1854; Hamilton to Toronto in December 1855; Galt to Guelph in 1857; Komoka to Sarnia in 1858, and finally the short spur line connecting Petrolia with Wyoming in 1866.

Modern locomotives are known simply by numbers, but in the 1850s those seen at the Hamilton station had been given names of African animals. There was "The Hippopotamus," "The Rhinocerus" and "The Elephant." These locomotives had been built in England. The next three were built in Hamilton by Mr. D.C. Gunn who gave them biblical names. Travellers were startled to see their train being pulled by "The Ham," "The Shem" and "Japhet."

Romance entered into the choice for the next series of locomotives, and mythological names were given, such as "Bacchus" and "The Achilles." Locomotives, especially during the steam era, were usually spoken of affectionately – somehow, it seems more suitable to call the object of your affection by name but today true railway enthusiasts become just as dewy-eyed when in hushed tones they speak of "Old 6218."

Despite the contribution the railway made to Hamilton's growth and prosperity, the frequency of railway accidents brought harsh criticism from people who were dissatisfied with safety standards.

Fires occurred frequently in the wooden coaches from careless use of the coal stoves and kerosene lamps but improvements were being brought about steadily.

Mr. A.F. Webster who was the depot agent when the old station was built in 1876, was present for the opening of the new building in 1931. On that occasion he marked that, "We all thought the new station was fine and afforded ample accommodation for years to come. Many were the complimentary remarks passed to and fro. Yet, now, Hamilton has one of the most handsome and best equipped stations on the continent. It is a credit to the city and to the Canadian National Railways, just as was the other many years ago."

Toronto Union Station

Haste and confusion, experienced so commonly among train passengers, dulls their perceptive powers, rendering them impervious to the charm and characteristics of their railway station.

The splendour of Toronto Union Station cannot be absorbed in full-flight – many unhurried visits are required to explore and discover its unique beauty. Like a fine painting, the station creates an individual interpretation for each viewer. You sense that the station honours the historic contribution made by the railways, and stands prepared to welcome the unknown.

Ever since the day when Lady Elgin officiated at the sod-turning ceremony of the Ontario, Simcoe and Huron Railway in 1851, close to the site of the present Toronto Union Station, it has become traditional for either nobility or royalty to be in attendance on similarly important occasions. When plans were being made for a suitable opening ceremony for Toronto's magnificent new Union Station, it was unanimously agreed that no one could impart greater prestige to the event than the idol of the British Empire, the Prince of Wales who later became Edward VIII. Torontonians who had waited for thirteen years to see the completion of their railway station were proud indeed when they filled the Great Hall of the Union Station on August 6, 1927 to witness the brief but impressive ceremony conducted by their popular Prince who concluded the formalities by stepping up to a ticket wicket to purchase the first railway ticket ever sold in this new railway station.

A tour of the Union Station should begin on Front Street where trees and gardens have been newly planted around the entrance ways, a delightful imitation of 19th century railway custom.

At the east portal of the station, a bronze plaque pays tribute to the first passenger train to leave Toronto. Beneath an embossed illustration of the train, "The Toronto," appears this proclamation,

> At this place on May 16, 1853
> the first train in Ontario
> hauled by a steam locomotive
> started and ran to Aurora.

Twenty-two massive stone columns rising to a height of forty feet form the grand entrance to the station. Each one was turned from solid Bedford Limestone, and their weight is over 75 tons.

The Great Hall (commonly called the Ticket Lobby) lives up to its name statistically – it is 250 feet long, 84 feet wide, with the ceiling 88 feet in height. In colour, texture and formation, the interior of the Hall is in such perfect harmony that no apparent line projects itself between the division of the vitrified Gustavino Tile of the arched ceiling, the walls of Zumbro stone, and the floors and stairways of Tennessee marble.

As one stands surveying the Hall, the eye is drawn immediately to the great arched windows at each end of the ticket lobby. Reflecting light from these windows suffuses the arched ceiling revealing the intricate details of its design. Carved in the stone frieze surrounding the room are the names of cities and towns on the lines of the Canadian National and Canadian Pacific Railways.

Two magnificent columns form the entrance to the departure concourse and through three ceiling-height windows framed by a low balustrade, shafts of sunlight illuminate the texture of the columns producing an almost iridescent quality in the light disseminating across the marble floor.

The formation of an invisible panorama at Toronto Union Station began on its opening day, with each piece of the mosaic being shaped by the moods and experiences of everyone who passed through the building. It is impossible to imagine any other public building being more weighted with memories of human emotions. During the depression years, scores of anxious men came by train to Toronto seeking employment, and for many of them the station became a haven. Throughout those trying years, summer months were still, however, happy times at the station when carefree families travelled to summer cottages, and young campers created sheer bedlam in the departure concourse with their shouting and shoving while weary camp counsellors tried to restore order. On Saturdays throughout the year, trails of confetti marked the way to the exit to the Niagara Falls train. In the late 1930s young men in military uniforms were a common sight at the station, and until 1945, troop trains carried thousands of Canada's men away from Toronto to points of overseas embarkation. Only those who lived through those tragic war years can ever really appreciate the deeply

emotional departures and homecomings which occurred at Union Station. At the conclusion of the Second World War every train from the East coast brought war-brides from Britain, and war-weary immigrants longing to become a part of this unscarred country.

The scene at Union Station changes constantly, and there have been, and always will be the battery of station loungers who never tire of watching the transition. Even though travelling habits and preferences have changed much to the detriment of railway passenger service, most Torontonians retain their great affection for the Union Station, and are united in the conviction that it must never be demolished.

A walk through the concourse can be a haunting experience for people who have known the station . . . memories, usually hidden in remote recesses of the mind, return with startling clarity. The rule which states that a house becomes a home only through its involvement with people, applies also to a railway station. It has taken over fifty years to make up the ever changing cast of Toronto Union Station. The station's redcaps have played an important role in this evolution and represent a bond between the old and the new. The clerks behind the ticket counters still perform their same duties, but here too, are changes. They no longer issue those wonderful long tickets which folded in accordion fashion, and seemed a pass to enchantment. Another change at the station is the absence of those remarkable ladies of the Travellers Aid whose compassionate acts of kindness often

produced miraculous results.

In the spirit of the season, the Toronto Union Station hospitably shares its good fortune with others at Christmas time. Throughout the week before Christmas, the joyful sound of carolling choirs and bands fills the Great Hall for the enjoyment of travellers. This feeling of intimacy has been maturing for over fifty years in the Union Station – it is the embodiment of an atmosphere created by the people who have journeyed to and from this place.

Toronto's Union Station stands today like a great monument to Ontario's railway history. All the trials of early railway builders . . . their courage, achievements and failures are assembled here to be honoured by this memorial.

Index